ANIMAL
TEACHINGS

ANIMAL TEACHINGS

ENHANCING OUR LIVES THROUGH THE WISDOM OF ANIMALS

DAWN BRUNKE

ILLUSTRATIONS BY OLA LIOLA

CICO BOOKS

LONDON NEW YORK

Published in 2012 by CICO Books
An imprint of Ryland Peters & Small Ltd
20–21 Jockey's Fields
London WC1R 4BW
519 Broadway, 5th Floor
New York, NY 10012

www.cicobooks.com

10 9 8 7 6 5 4 3 2 1

A CIP catalog record for this book is available from
the Library of Congress and the British Library.

ISBN: 978 1 908170 41 5

Printed in China

Illustrator: Ola Liola

Editor: Marion Paull
Design concept: Paul Tilby
Designer: Jerry Goldie

For digital editions, visit
www.cicobooks.com/apps.php

Contents

Animal Groups:

What Are Animal Teachings?

Once upon a time, humans and animals shared a common language. Our ancestors conversed fluently with Raven and Bear, Turtle and Whale. We understood each other, freely expressing our thoughts, feelings, and observations; and since we recognized that everything was meaningful and essential, we listened to nature. We sensed our unity with all beings and celebrated diversity through sharing our distinctive ways of living.

Animals had much to share with us. Fox taught us to survey our surroundings without being seen; Tiger, how to focus our attention; and with Spider, we sat spellbound, sensing the ancient wisdom of creation weaving reality. By listening carefully, we learned not only how to survive but also how to thrive. We received sage advice and discovered some secrets, too.

How did we stray so far from this intimate connection with the natural world, this joyful celebration of life? Why did we separate from our fellow animals, creating an "us" and "them"? At times, we even told ourselves that animals were dumb, soulless creatures. Thus we lost much of our heart connection.

Our exploration of what it means to be human has been a tremendous, but costly, learning. As we developed exclusive forms of language, culture, religion, and technology, we valued "our" perspectives above others, so detaching ourselves further from the natural world.

Early shamans—medicine men, wise women—intuitively sought animals as guides to the sacred. To call upon an animal's power was to connect with the animal's spirit. By wearing feathers, bones, claws, or hide, by singing its song or imitating its movement, the shaman embodied an animal's wisdom, partaking of its medicine or abilities. Some humans formed alliances with animals, working at deeper levels to return those teachings to the community, back into our collective memory.

How to Communicate with Animals

Step One: Calm Down

Our minds chatter as we make plans, divert our thoughts, multitask, and try to control our world. Unfortunately, this habit keeps us just skimming along the surface of awareness. To really hear animals (and ourselves), we need to calm down. We need to sink deep, beyond the superficial. We need to quiet ourselves, letting go of inner talk, expectations, judgments and ideas of how things should be. So, breathe deep! Clear a space within yourself. Luxuriate in the calm and quiet center of your being.

Step Two: Open Up

As we shake loose from our habitual ways of experiencing the world, we become more aware of our feelings, more perceptive, more sensitive to the way things really are. Animals generally read character. In acknowledging who we are, right here, right now, we open ourselves to honest communication. In short, we show up for life. Present, attentive, and curious, we are then able to welcome the unfolding of relationship.

Step Three: Listen Deep

We experience the world through our senses, as do animals. When we ask a question, animals may respond by sharing their opinions or unique world experiences through feelings, images, dialogue, or even joined consciousness.

We may see a scene unfolding within our mind, hear an animal's thoughts, sense emotions, or feel physical sensations. The universal communication device that we all possess creatively translates any experience, linking speaker and listener intimately, enhancing mutual understanding and appreciation.

Every communication holds an opening to deeper relationship. Trust yourself. You will know when you are connected. If you need help, just ask. Most animals find ways to nudge our abilities, jump-start our creativity, and help streamline our translation process, especially when we are sincere and attentive.

So, relax, explore, have fun. As we open our heart and mind to learn more about others, we also learn more about ourselves. We learn to listen and hear and feel, and, as a result, to connect with the deeper aspects of who we are. And so we join ourselves with animals in celebration.

Forming Animal Alliances

This is a book of co-creation, a gathering of humans and animals in mutual cooperation. I was often surprised by what animals had to say, and honored by the depth of their sharing.

Sometimes, in my human way, I would first research and write about an animal species, collecting information from mythology, traditional teachings, wildlife observations, science, art, dreams, and literary references—observing, wondering, dissecting, analyzing, deliberating, musing, pondering. But my favorite part was opening to animal groups, asking for their input or teaching. In some cases, I felt animal energy while researching, sensing the excitement or eagerness of a group wanting to contribute or, in some cases, clarify. Other times, animals volunteered to speak first, to set the record straight before I had a chance to do my human digging.

This is one example of how we can form alliances with animals—in this case, a writer and many groups of animals finding a way to share teachings with other humans, with you.

The illustrator of this book, Ola Liola, experienced a similar deepening and connection to animals while drawing. As the project progressed, she wrote to me, "I feel not only a connection to an animal as I draw, but the painting process helps me deepen and get closer to understanding its essence. First it happened with cats. After I started to draw such independent animals, I slowly fell in love with them. I was not connected to them because all my life I lived with dogs. Cat was, for me, very distant. But by drawing and painting cats I found a similarity in our behavior, and now associate some features with myself. Each time I work with a new animal I feel a closeness; I feel how it enriches me. Sometimes I compare myself with these animals and feel like I have a part of each of them in my subconscious."

Animal guides, power animals, totem animals, and animal teachers—these terms can all refer to the energetic presence of an animal group. Sometimes when we work with animal teachers, we draw upon the larger dimensions of animal energy or spirit. But animal teachings come through physical animals as well, often in unusual and unexpected ways. The question is, are we listening?

One morning, shortly after I had pruned my list of animal contributors for this book, a robin tapped insistently at a window pane, waking my husband and me. My husband shooed it away, but the persistent robin flew to another window and tapped again. Suddenly, I realized that I had cut Robin from the list, and this bird wanted *in*. So I went to the computer, added Robin, and the bird stopped tapping. Later, while researching the species, I discovered that Robin inspires new endeavors, boosts creativity, and teaches us about the wisdom of change.

Animal teachers come for many reasons. Some work with us for a lifetime. These animals generally speak to our spiritual nature, reminding us of long-range goals and overall life teachings.

Other animals come for a particular period of time, perhaps as we face a specific challenge or adventure. Sometimes several animals show up, bearing distinct yet related teaching to encourage or remind us. When we finish our lesson, our teacher moves on. We may even receive a graduation message as a sign of completion.

Still other animals show up as messengers. Their teaching pertains to the moment, and may signal a passing opportunity, or help us to decide, if we are at a crossroads. Such messengers may bring clarity or advise caution—a nudge to stop, an encouragement to leap, or a flash of spiritual insight.

Lastly, some animal teachers help with shadow material, revealing repressed fears or issues that trigger our darker emotions. Shadow teachers sometimes test us to determine whether we are ready for their medicine. Working with shadow teachers is not always easy, but it can be very rewarding. Shadow animals are among our most powerful guides.

Animal teachers, helpers, advisors, partners, and friends are all around us, all the time. If we remain alert and aware, open to learning through honest relationship, we can enjoy the many benefits and wonders that animal alliances bring. The animal world calls us home, in love.

GROUP 1
Attention & Awareness

GIRAFFE ~ MOUSE ~ RABBIT ~ RACCOON ~ TIGER

Attention and awareness—two distinct but complementary ways of knowing—help us to experience ourselves and understand our world.

To pay attention means to take notice. It involves concentration and careful observation. Initially, we may be curious or captivated, but then, senses sharply tuned, we aim and focus our perception, directing it to a specific target. When we come to attention, we are alert, intense, on guard, like a cat ready to pounce.

When our awareness comes into play, we spontaneously sense what we are doing or feeling. Awareness tends to be comprehensive and inclusive, and we can be aware of many things at once: noises, sensations, emotions, earthy smells, and explosions of taste. Awareness allows us to be present, conscious of ourselves in the now.

Attention is purposeful, a deliberate focus of intention, while awareness rolls open, unfurling, often without a particular emphasis. Attention is directed, coming mainly from our mind; awareness is a flow of feeling through our heart and being. Think of awareness as the ocean and attention the boat. Awareness is the floodlight, attention the laser beam.

With attention and awareness, we filter our sensory experiences. We can focus and fine tune our attention to distinguish, discern, and alert us to danger, and we can broaden our awareness to feel from afar. But it's all a balance. Too much focus and we can get mired in details. Too much free flowing of the senses and we may get lost in the everywhere of everything.

By being attentive and aware, we can develop flexibility in consciousness and increase our range of knowing. We can both dig deep and open wide. Zooming in with pin-pointed, crystal clarity, we can identify, analyze, and comprehend. Zooming out, we can expand sensory experience beyond our physical presence to exercise our intuition and embrace larger dimensions of being.

At home in ourselves, attentive and aware, our consciousness blossoms and thrives.

ANIMAL TEACHERS OF ATTENTION & AWARENESS

GIRAFFE ~ *As the tallest land mammal, Giraffe links earth with sky, reminding us to balance spiritual wisdom with grounded awareness, and to live in the present while keeping an attentive eye on the future.*

MOUSE ~ *Curious, watchful, and with expert attention to detail, Mouse reminds us to examine the little things in life and be aware of our environment.*

RABBIT ~ *Although often quiet and reserved, Rabbit is a keen observer, who can surprise with hidden teachings. Rabbit encourages us to peer beneath the surface and trust ourselves as we face our deeper fears.*

RACCOON ~ *Naturally curious and observant, with a penchant for exploration, Raccoon exposes deception and reveals what hides behind the masks of others and ourselves.*

TIGER ~ *A fine example of disciplined attention and authority, Tiger helps us to remove distractions of the mind, awaken passion, and center our presence in the here and now.*

Giraffe

Feet on the earth and head in the sky, Giraffe—the tallest land animal on our planet—offers a link between worlds, a bridge between practicality and spiritual insight.

Owing to its great height, good hearing, and keen vision, Giraffe senses what is coming. Giraffe's expansive vantage point can help us to see into the distance—and into the future. Giraffe encourages us to find balance in our views: to be well grounded and live in the present while remaining alert and attentive to where we are headed. In this way, we can move forward with confidence.

Giraffes live in herds and depend upon family and community for protection and survival. Giraffe helps us to have strong, loving relationships.

Giraffe's long, slender neck (made up of seven vertebrae, just as in humans) is both sturdy and flexible. Giraffe reminds us to look in all directions and consider different points of view. Giraffe may also prompt us to stick our neck out or extend ourselves—to reach higher than we thought possible. Giraffe reveals how to be supple in our bodies, adaptable in our viewpoints, and expansive in our intuitive awareness.

Generally quiet, giraffes often use stares and neck and tail movements to communicate. Giraffe reminds us to pay attention to visual cues, to be aware of refined body language, and not to say too much or too little. Giraffe also teaches the importance of silence and how to find pleasure in quiet contemplation, and so is an excellent guide to relaxed meditation.

Giraffe motivates us to link awareness with attention by maintaining a grounded outlook that is also broad and expansive. When things feel out of reach, Giraffe can help.

GIRAFFE SAYS

We love our children and the earth. We enjoy our bright, open skies. Our height reminds us to stay in equilibrium with ourselves, not to lean too far one way or another.

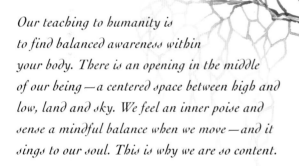

Our teaching to humanity is to find balanced awareness within your body. There is an opening in the middle of our being—a centered space between high and low, land and sky. We feel an inner poise and sense a mindful balance when we move—and it sings to our soul. This is why we are so content.

We invite you to share in our stability, to feel the centeredness of our strength as we adapt to each new moment. Perhaps you, too, may feel the joy of open space and deep, contented peace.

We send our greetings so that you may find this awareness within yourselves. We are Giraffe.

Mouse

Small and scrupulous, Mouse is a natural investigator and detective. Tucked into tiny hiding holes, Mouse knows how to use smallness to its advantage and observe life from a place of safety.

Mice have keen senses and use their sensitive whiskers to feel where they are going. Mouse helps us to be aware of our environment, even in the dark, and to sense a situation fully before acting.

Quick and nimble, mice love to explore and scrutinize, but they also have a keen knack for evading obstacles. Mouse encourages us to be daring in our travels and explorations—but not too daring. For Mouse also cautions us to be alert and watchful of danger.

Mouse understands double meanings and prompts us to consider both the pros and cons of a situation. Mouse helps us to focus our attention on the little things that need to be done so that we can achieve big things. With Mouse we learn to organize our thoughts and review our options.

Attention to details is key, for Mouse shows how what initially seems small or insignificant may prove to have larger meaning and purpose later on. Mouse reminds us to examine the fine print before making decisions, and not to jump into situations too quickly.

Then again, too much Mouse energy and we may get lost in trivia, failing to see the larger picture, and never move forward at all. Be careful when partaking of Mouse medicine—a little goes a long way.

Mouse is quiet, discreet, and quickly adaptable. It is ironic that tiny Mouse can evoke sizable fear in humans. In Indian mythology, it is Mouse who carries the great elephant-headed god, Ganesh, upon its back. Such is the power of the small.

MOUSE SAYS

Yes, we are small, but we are strong and carry a large medicine. We are good friends who know how to listen carefully. We often work with children, helping them to hide and find safety. We are willing to work with humans in a more conscious way. All you have to do is ask, and Mouse will help.

We mostly work with humans behind the scenes, between the cracks, in small ways that have large consequences. Think of the outline of an angle. We are the tiny dot in the center, but the extent of our range (both physically and metaphysically) is the outward projection of that angle. We understand how the small is the start of the large, how the seed is the start of the tree.

We offer humanity a reminder: by honoring the small, the large will unfold smoothly, for the benefit of all.

Rabbit

Sensitive, quick-thinking, spontaneous and unpredictable, Rabbit is a keen observer who is fast and agile. Rabbit understands the power of invisibility, knowing when to flee and when to freeze in the presence of danger.

Rabbit teaches us to be alert to our feelings, attentive to our intuition, and aware of our surroundings. In this way, we can sense the optimum timing of opportunity, knowing when to wait and when to leap, and how to speed up plans already put in motion.

On the surface, rabbits may seem to be timid and fearful, but Rabbit has an affinity for paradox—and hidden teachings. Who would suspect that soft, quiet, gentle Rabbit is a powerful guide to the shadow world? If we are willing to peer beneath the surface, Rabbit will help, leading us down, underground, to discover the dark subconscious fears that choke and hold us captive.

With Rabbit as mentor, we learn to move through fear by using our wits and trusting our intuition. Rabbit reminds us not to allow apprehensive thoughts to multiply—for projecting alarm and panic only brings to us the very things we fear. Rabbit encourages us to bring our fright into the light, helping us to face our fears with love and compassion for ourselves.

Rabbit reveals a peaceful joy. Associated with good luck and happiness, Rabbit also speaks of health, fertility, abundance, and fortune. Rabbit is connected with the fairy realm and can help us to notice magic in the world. There is a reason why it is Rabbit who comes out of the magician's hat.

RABBIT SAYS

In the past, much of our wisdom was couched in myth and story, but we are working more directly with humans these days. We sense many humans concealing their darker thoughts and emotions beneath the surface of their being.

We Rabbits urge you to lighten up—to be honest with yourself as you investigate who you are. Great gold lies in facing your fears, in taking a long look at what holds you and keeps you tied to the underground aspect of your being.

In former times, Rabbits were associated with the moon, and we are sometimes pictured leaping into the moon. This is because we possess an energy of flight and lunar light.

Our advice to humans is to retrieve your dark pieces, and to love those pieces as you would love your children, for they are also a part of you. The more you do this, the lighter you will become. Perhaps you will become light enough to leap with us Rabbits and know the joy of a lightened heart.

Raccoon

Easily identified by its distinctive dark mask, Raccoon is a good-natured trickster who can outsmart and mislead. Raccoon knows how to deceive, and how to discern trickery in others. Raccoon can also help us to discover our own disguises of self-deception.

Mostly nocturnal and naturally inquisitive, raccoons delight in adventures and exploration. With sensitive, dexterous paws, they twist off lids, pry up latches, open windows, and turn door-knobs. Familiar with the ways of humans, raccoons readily help themselves to food and shelter. Too much Raccoon energy can lead to trouble.

Raccoons are good observers and easily adapt to new situations. Raccoon medicine helps us to loosen up, be more observant, and engage the spirit of curiosity. Raccoon can be secretive and identify secrets in others. Not much escapes Raccoon's attention.

Raccoon is a master of exposing disguise, helping us to recognize masks, and reminding us that life is not always as it seems. Raccoon also teaches that there is much to be gained by trying on masks, for each reveals a different perspective on life. By wearing an animal mask, for example, we may explore the medicine and power of that animal, even sharing its awareness and perceiving in new ways.

Raccoon shows us how to use a mask to our advantage, how to change a mask to fit the situation, and how to discard those we have outgrown. As we release the many masks of ego, Raccoon turns our awareness to spiritual deepening.

Raccoon medicine is often long-term—not a quick fix, but a learning process. When we are ready, Raccoon can help us to change. Meeting Raccoon may indicate that we are ready to face ourselves, or that our true self will soon be revealed.

RACCOON SAYS

We are gentle creatures.
We can be fierce in defending ourselves or protecting our children,
but we are mostly easy-going and fascinated by life.

On basic levels, we find comfort in warm, dry bedding and good food. We know how to be aware of opportunity—everything you need is available if only you look! We invite you to try on "Raccoon eyes" to perceive the bounty of life.

We are clever and we like to work with humans who are curious and want to explore. We can help you to get out of boxed, boring ways of seeing the world. We like to dig around and search out secrets.

Our advice to humanity is to see beyond the apparent. And if you need a bit of fun and adventure, come romp with us. We can see in the dark and know how to party.

Tiger

FOCUS ~ PRESENCE ~ PASSION ~ CONFIDENCE ~ DISCIPLINE ~ DEVOTION

Solitary and silent, stealthy hunter of the night, Tiger's focus is on the here and now. Razor-sharp claws are hidden within tigers' powerful paws, but tigers use restraint, control their emotions, and strike only when necessary. Tiger understands timing—and thus enjoys success.

Tiger teaches the importance of concentration, patience, and how to use the element of surprise. With Tiger, we learn to release mental distractions and be more consciously aware. Tiger's intensity demands that we be fully present.

Tiger is not so much about play, but purpose. However, Tiger awakens passion, readying us for new adventures. When Tiger shows up, we may sense a renewed response to life—ardent, intense, eager— not just halfway, but fully and passionately. Tiger energy is strong, emotionally deep. We *feel* with Tiger, moving sleekly, furtively through the jungle of our self.

Each tiger's stripes are unique, and their majestic style reveals the balance in Tiger: calm yet energized, clear and focused yet fully aware. Revered by Buddhists for disciplined aware- ness and devotion, Tiger is linked to enlightenment.

Tiger medicine urges us to gain self-control, temper personal magnetism, and use will-power without manipulation. To work with Tiger means to come into our own authority. Tiger inspires us to focus our awareness and walk our path with independence, confidence, and a healthy sense of self.

When Tiger comes to call, we are asked to awaken our senses, follow our passion, and center ourselves in the moment.

TIGER SAYS

We are truth-tellers. We walk our path without excuses. Every step is deliberate, focused in the present. We are about being who we are. This is a teaching we offer to humans, who sometimes hide behind ways they think they should be or want to be. We face life head on, present in our body, luxuriating in the full knowledge of ourselves.

We are aware of our presence on earth not only as individual, unique tigers but as conscious embodiments of Tiger essence. In this way, we align physicality with soul.

We encourage direction—not from a mental point of view, but by feeling the flow of life through our bodies. Thus we enjoy the precision of right timing, and become one with the grace of movement. We can narrow our attention to the smallest detail, yet know our place and feel at home in the immensity of any jungle.

We offer help when you have a difficult road ahead. We offer persistence, forward movement, direction, and reclamation of your own true self. We are Tiger.

Balance

CAMEL ~ COW ~ PENGUIN ~ PRAIRIE DOG ~ WOLF

Balance tells us that all is well. A balanced life is calm and steady, not obsessive or overly anxious. In balance, we feel our connection with the natural flow of life. We are in the moment, at home in ourselves. We can rejoice in whatever comes, responding with spontaneity, drawing upon our innate wisdom, our treasury of abilities. Trusting our inner balance, we can fearlessly try on new ideas.

We often find balance in movement. On a bicycle, we balance ourselves by pedaling and coasting, not by standing still. Walking, swimming, dancing, surfing—the momentum in all these brings a physical response to help us balance. We find balance not in stasis but in the flow of life. We can physically feel ourselves balancing as we adapt and adjust, making major modifications or minute shifts. With a balanced perspective, we flow with the changing cycles of life and groove with the currents of living.

Finding mental balance often involves letting go of what we think we know and opening up to what is. In balance, we give up rigid control. Even when tousled by the ups and downs, high and lows, and crazy turnarounds of living, we can find balance by grounding, attuning with the earth, sensing the intrinsic harmony of life. Balance enables us to hold steady, finding stability and equilibrium in our body, mind, and spirit. A balanced life has everything in proper proportion—not too much, not too little. Balance reminds us to alternate work with rest, solitude with togetherness.

Balance is an inner compass, a point of reference that helps us to center and remember who we are. A self in balance is not so much about outer appearances as how we feel inside.

With enlightened balance, we join the diverse aspects of our many selves: curious child and wise elder, artist and scholar, scientist and magician. In balance with others, we sense our underlying unity yet celebrate our diversity. Balance is the open heart, the center of the diamond, the flow of life coursing through us.

ANIMAL TEACHERS OF BALANCE

CAMEL ~ *As an ancient species able to traverse vast deserts, Camel knows how to balance space and time in order to endure. Camel reminds us how to adapt and find balance within so that we can go the distance.*

COW ~ *Gentle and sensitive, in peaceful connection with family and pasture, herd and Mother Earth, Cow sees the goodness in life and offers the balanced teaching of contentment.*

PENGUIN ~ *With agility and grace, Penguin bridges the worlds of water and land, showing us how to move fluidly between realities and find balance in our perspective on life.*

PRAIRIE DOG ~ *Outgoing, curious, efficient, and organized, Prairie Dog knows how to balance work with play, and how to create harmonious order within a large group.*

WOLF ~ *Intelligent and perceptive, loyal and loving, Wolf helps us to balance freedom with responsibility, and to walk our path with integrity.*

Camel

BALANCES TIME AND SPACE ~ SURVIVES THE LONG HAUL ~
ADAPTS AND ENDURES

Unpredictable, yet patient and intelligent, Camel demonstrates how to survive well in harsh environments by finding balance within. Camels are well known for their ability to cross vast expanses of hot desert sands, even while carrying heavy loads. Camel helps us to conserve energy and to discover unexpected stamina as we persist and endure.

Camels' ancient connection to long-distance travel comes from their ability to keep going for a long time with just a little water. Long eyelashes and closing nostrils protect them from sand storms, and broad feet enable them to walk over shifting terrain. Camel offers protection and can teach us how to transform burdens and lighten our load, especially during journeys of great range or over harsh ground. Camel knows how to balance time and space, and has learned to adapt. Camel reminds us that we, too, can survive.

Camels' humps (dromedary or Arabian camels have two, Bactrian camels have one) store energy, and specialized metabolism allows conservation of water. Camel medicine can help us to regulate our metabolism, pace ourselves, and keep our energy levels on an even keel. If we are parched, Camel offers assistance.

The appearance of Camel may indicate that a difficult journey or tough times lie ahead, but Camel also reminds us that we have the fortitude to succeed. Camel inspires us to accomplish what seems difficult or even impossible, and to trust that things will work out.

Camels sleep very little, and only for short periods of time. A power nap with Camel can quickly restore balance. Camel helps us to replenish ourselves, to survive in difficult situations, and to endure the long haul. Call upon Camel for extra energy reserves.

CAMEL SAYS

We are tough and we endure. Our teaching is about persistence and finding balance within to persevere. We place one foot in front of the other, and that is how we can move anywhere, through anything. Small steps lead to great distance. This is a truth we know.

We envision ourselves in a long line stretching through time and space. In each step, we feel an opening to the past, sensing camels who have walked this way before. In each step, we see the long line of camel-kind stretching from here to there.

In this way, we draw upon what has gone before and what will come, and what we are a part of now. Thus we find our balance in the shifting sands of time and space. We are Camel and we welcome you to share our teaching, to discover this sense of balanced connection within yourself.

Cow

PEACE ~ PATIENCE ~ CONTENTMENT ~ SERENITY

Soulful eyes and quiet intelligence reflect Cow's caring, giving nature. Cow is about finding peace in the pasture, being at home with one's family, in close connection with the earth. The teaching of balance that Cow offers is contentment.

Calm and generous, cows know how to share with their herd. Cow can help to settle and ground erratic energies. Cow teaches us to be easy-going and live in the present, and to find a happy, balanced sense of self.

Cows provide nutrition through their milk, not only to calves but to humans as well. A giver of life and protector of children, Cow teaches nurturance and motherly devotion. While Bull energy is bold and masculine, Cow energy is soft and feminine. Bull is a symbol of the sun and Cow a symbol of the moon. Together, Bull and Cow symbolize fertility, abundance, and a balance of male and female energies.

Cow has several lunar connections. Moon goddesses once wore the horns of cows upon their heads. As young children, we learn that Cow jumps over the moon. But Cow is also connected with the earth and thus offers a balance between lunar rhythms and terrestrial stability. Cow is an aspect of the Divine Mother, the Great Nourisher, from whom flows streams of milk, offering sustenance to all.

Gentle, sensitive, tranquil, and at ease, Cow sees the goodness of life. However, Cow can also sense danger—often before other farm animals.

Cow teaches patience and, with gentle persistence, prompts us to shift potential into possibility. Cow can motivate and encourage when we begin a project, and offers a balanced overview of what is needed. Loving and altruistic, Cow calmly shares insight and serenity.

COW SAYS

We like to graze and wander in close connection with the earth. We love to feel ourselves in communion with our young and each other. We sense a gentle pulse flowing through our herd that reverberates inside our bodies and connects us all.

Our advice to humans is to slow down, feel the ground beneath your feet, smell the grassy fields, settle yourself in shared community. We offer the teaching of patience, of thoroughly digesting experiences before you react. We bring calmness. We accept even those things that feel alien to our being.

We are like the earth, protective and supportive. Our counsel is to remember you are a part of life and connected to us, even if you do not see it to be so. We sense deeply and know the love that flows through all. We invite you to feel it inside yourself. We are Cow and we love you all.

Penguin

There is a puzzle about penguins. These are birds who use their wings as fins to swim, rather than to fly. But there is a practicality about penguins as well. Their dark backs blend with water when viewed from above, and their white under-bellies blend with sky light when seen from below. Penguin's elegant camouflage, along with the ability to be at home in different worlds, hints at the teaching of balance.

Penguins have poor vision, a bad sense of smell, and can be clumsy on land. In the water, however, penguins swim with grace and ease. Penguin knows how to bridge realities, balancing awkwardness in one world with agility and expertise in another. Penguin boosts self-confidence by encouraging us to accept both our strengths and weaknesses, and so feel more at home in the world.

An amazing talent to leap from the sea and land upright demonstrates penguins' expertise at making swift transitions. Penguin shows how to navigate deftly between different environments.

Often associated with astral projection and waking dreams, Penguin reveals how to move fluidly from one dimension to another. Penguin can guide us in linking dream states with waking consciousness, shifting realities, and finding balance between the hidden and the known.

In keeping with their formal "tuxedo" look, mated penguins bow to one another. Indeed, much about penguin behavior is proper and orderly. Penguin can help us to adapt and develop socially, be it in terms of good manners or respect for ourselves and others.

The appearance of Penguin may alert us to upcoming changes, hinting that we may need to alter our outlook. But all is well, for Penguin is purposeful and can help us to find a more balanced perspective on life.

Wolf says

We are Wolf, fast of foot, sharp of mind. We speak to the deeper part of your self and soul. We can move silently, furtively, through the shadow of your being.

Humans have projected much onto wolves. We have been feared and hated, worshipped and revered. We reflect to you what you see about yourself. We are at home within ourselves. This is the main teaching we offer humanity at this time.

Yes, we are demanding—we see clearly and ask you to do the same.

We love our children and offer them wisdom, knowing they are the future pack. In a similar way, we work with humans, helping you to traverse shadows, face your fears, and find yourself. To align self and spirit is a powerful undertaking. This is the teaching of balance that we carry.

We are wild and devoted, dedicated yet free. We are Wolf, and we live within you as well.

Communication

BADGER ~ COYOTE ~ ELEPHANT ~ MONKEY ~ RAVEN

Communication stems from our universal need to share. With good communication, we can exchange ideas, convey knowledge, impart feelings, give advice, and pass on secrets. Communication connects and joins, linking sender to receiver, face to face or through space and time. For example, an author writes, not knowing who will read the work, or where or when. People from ancient cultures speak to us through drawings, statues, hieroglyphics, and the mysteries of their dead.

Fireflies glow with light and octopuses change the colored pattern of their skin; eels pulse electric waves and ants secrete invisible trails of coded information—all to communicate. Like other animals, humans employ many forms of communication—speaking, singing, dancing, flirting, laughing, loving. We can articulate feelings and thoughts with movements, expressions, gestures, and posture. Indeed, body language often reveals more than words express, and sometimes we inadvertently expose our hidden emotions.

Birds display colors and dogs wag their tails; we smile, squint, grimace, or shrug to let our feelings be known. Dolphins click, chickens cluck, ravens shriek, and alligators rumble, each species broadcasting its specialized calls. We groom and sniff and rub and stroke, using touch to relay sentiments that are deeper than words. Life on earth offers a rich diversity of communication—so many ways to learn about others and ourselves!

Humans have developed complex spoken and written languages. We transmit ideas *en masse* through media and film. We can telegraph and telephone, telecast and telecommute. We can confer instantly with almost anyone, anywhere, through the ubiquitous presence of the Internet. It is an outward, uniquely human manifestation of something other animals use naturally—for the Inner-net is the universal form of communication that truly connects us all.

In celebrating the songs of life, we deepen in connection. Heart to heart, soul to soul, we engage the universal language—the timeless, silent form of conversing—and in the still center of communication, we commune.

ANIMAL TEACHERS OF COMMUNICATION

BADGER ~ *Tough and brave, Badger helps us to be assertive and articulate our opinions with clarity and strong persuasion.*

COYOTE ~ *As the consummate trickster, Coyote communicates wisdom through humor and reminds us to laugh at ourselves.*

ELEPHANT ~ *Gentle, loyal, and loving, Elephant knows how to listen with understanding, engage telepathy, and respond to life with sensitivity and inner knowing.*

MONKEY ~ *A quick mind and flexible attitude enable Monkey to inspire creativity in communication.*

RAVEN ~ *Linked to the spirit world as a messenger and guide, Raven awakens intuition, brings depth and clarity to communication, and offers powerful medicine to those who are ready to transform themselves.*

Badger

Bold, brave, and sometimes aggressive, Badger offers powerful medicine. Badgers are compact and well muscled, and can be fierce, especially if cornered. They have sharp claws, tough skin, and strong jaws, and they know how to defend themselves, putting up a ferocious fight when necessary.

Badgers have an excellent sense of hearing and of smell. Badger knows how to listen and can sniff out the deeper truth. Despite poor eyesight, Badger has a keen sense of inner sight and can help us to see beneath appearances.

Badgers are amazing diggers and burrowers. They live underground. When too much is going on, Badger reminds us to sink down, ground ourselves, and focus. Delving beneath the surface, Badger uncovers the secrets we hold within.

Badger feels at home with earth energies. Observing plant and animal spirits of the lower world, Badger collects and organizes vast knowledge and resources. As a keeper of earth stories, Badger protects ancient wisdom and guards the truth.

Badger's strong jaws and independent attitude champion self-expression. Badger medicine pushes us to speak up, with honesty, be assertive, and ask for what we want. Too much Badger, however, may cause us to speak too quickly, too sharply, without concern for others or thought of consequence.

With Badger at our side, we will not back down. Badger's tenacity inspires us to state our opinion, explain our point of view, and persuade and convince, even if it requires creative use of volatile emotions. Badger energy is potent—a little goes a long way.

Working with Badger is not easy. Badger demands respect, but is fair and trustworthy. Badger urges us to change what needs to be changed. Badger energy is helpful for those who are submissive, stuck, or apathetic.

BADGER SAYS

We don't work with many humans, but those who receive our invitation find us serious and exacting teachers.

We burrow down to commune with the earth and her many mysteries. We see within and that is our expertise in communication. We can dig down to the core of things, helping you to discover what you really want to know.

We like our place in the earth; we are a grounded and sensitive species. If you come to us, we may ask you to sit awhile. You can observe us and we can observe you. This is an opening to communication. This is how we work. Yes, we dive in—deeply at times—but we also know the value of getting to know others by sensing their energy.

We require honesty in communication. We are practical and don't waste time by thinking what could be or should be. Our focus is seeing what is.

Coyote

Smart and cunning, an accomplished trickster and amazing survivor, Coyote knows how to laugh at life. Acute senses, keen instincts, and good problem-solving skills enable coyotes to adapt to almost any environment. Flexible and creative, Coyote accepts what comes and makes the best of it.

Coyotes come and go, living in loosely structured family groups. When one coyote howls at the moon, those nearby respond in chorus. Coyote encourages joyous outbursts of spontaneity. With Coyote, we can find our authentic voice and learn to sing with abandon.

When Coyote shows up, it's a hint that things are not quite as they seem. Clever and discerning, Coyote notices when we are off our path. Skirting around the shadows of our being, Coyote holds up a mirror, nudging us to see what is really there, and thus discover a deeper sense of self.

In nature, coyotes use diversionary tactics to confuse and fascinate their prey. In myth, Coyote teases, lies, exaggerates, and cajoles, tricking others into letting down their guard and then—*zing!* Coyote often plays the fool to show how easily we fool ourselves, but balances unorthodox humor with knowledge and skill. Coyote has a knack for guiding us back into alignment—not only with ourselves but also with others, reminding us that we are all in this together.

Coyote advises us not to take things too seriously. By laughing at ourselves we open up to a powerful form of healing. Coyote urges us to trust our instincts and take a risk, for even if it does not pay off, we can find wisdom through experience.

Enthusiastic, inventive, adventurous, and resourceful, Coyote brings out our childlike curiosity, prompting us to lighten up and enjoy. Coyote helps us to speak our truth and fully embrace our own selves. With Coyote we learn to expect—and grasp—the unexpected.

COYOTE SAYS

We coyotes have had a wild ride with humans. You have not always treated us well, although some of your kind have honored and revered us. We shine when you tell our tales, for all coyotes sense the trickster Coyote living within.

We advocate taking it easy, but always being on guard, alert to opportunity. We encourage clever wisdom—seeing the little things that hold everything together. We have finely tuned senses and we enjoy using them. If you come to work with us, this is level one: learning to fine tune your sensing apparatus.

We like to work with humans who know how to laugh and have a good time. But we are not lazy. We love to explore and learn new things. With an open mind, you can see what's really present and sniff out openings for fun and learning. That's the Coyote way of life!

Elephant

Strong, dignified, and intelligent, Elephant is an ancient symbol of royalty, wisdom, and the warrior spirit. Elephant feels deeply and responds to life with attuned inner knowing.

Elephants smell, taste, touch, and communicate with their extremely versatile and sensitive trunk. They also have a unique ability to communicate over long distances using low-frequency sounds, and so are linked to telepathy. Their large, flapping ears remind us to listen carefully. Elephant can help us to deepen our listening skills, develop telepathic abilities, and discern the subtleties of nonverbal communication.

Elephants and humans display many similar emotions, from joy and love to grief and rage. Living in groups led by a wise and loving matriarch, elephants form deep bonds with each other and are devoted mothers. They protect the collective wisdom of their species by passing herd knowledge to their young with patience, care, and affection. Elephant nurtures wisdom and teaches us to be more effective in our dealings with others by using gentleness and compassion.

Elephants remember well, and can carry a grudge. However, Elephant is a perceptive guide, showing us how to dig through old memories, uncover what is hidden, and bring it to the surface for healing.

Stable and determined, Elephant is often associated with removing obstacles. In the wild, elephants can knock down almost anything, due to their size and strength. Elephant energy is steadfast, although too much can be reckless and bulldozing.

Elephant values commitment, loyalty, and heartfelt communication. Elephant helps us to be patient, and may remind us of our responsibility to family, especially in caring for children and elders. Elephant teaches us to love our family and cherish our herd.

ELEPHANT SAYS

Although we have strong, solid bodies, we have gentle hearts and sensitive souls. Our time with humans has not always been easy, but we keep the connection open, hoping you will hear our deeper thoughts and feel our desire to join with you in a way that benefits all.

We love our children and to be with our herd. We know you love the same. Our walk on the earth is a deepening in togetherness. By walking with our kind, we connect with all elephants, from all times and places, even those who no longer reside on earth.

Our teaching to humanity is to slow down and listen. Less words, more feeling; less doing, more presence.

Trunk to tail, we elephants form a ring around the earth. We hold the earth close to us because we love her, and we love you as well. Listen deeply and love. That is our call to you.

Monkey

CREATIVE ~ PLAYFUL ~ INQUISITIVE ~ AWAKENS CURIOSITY AND INTROSPECTION

Agile, acrobatic, and full of energy, Monkey has a quick mind and is an excellent communicator. Monkey conveys information clearly and creatively through body gestures, grooming, loose-limbed movements, long-distance shrieks, throaty howls, and other specialized vocalizations.

Monkeys love to play, socialize, and explore. Watching other animals, they imitate actions and sounds, including those of humans. Open-minded and inquisitive, Monkey converses with nature spirits. Monkey reveals how to develop nimble thought by considering new ways of seeing, appreciating different perspectives of life and adjusting our point of view. For this reason, Monkey often symbolizes "right living" on earth.

There are over 250 species of monkeys living in many different environments—from jungles and grasslands to mountains, and displaying varying physical forms—the tiny pygmy marmoset, the brightly colored mandrill, the very loud howler monkey. This indicates adaptability, innovation, and resourcefulness, and Monkey's relationship with humans is just as flexible—from pets to laboratory animals, from space explorers to service animals.

Naturally curious and sometimes mischievous, Monkey encourages us to see both the dark and light of a situation. By doing so, we may discover something about ourselves. Monkeys can be lighthearted and funny, but Monkey also helps us to connect with the deeper recesses of our self.

Intelligent problem-solvers subject to a wide range of emotions, most monkeys know how to balance aggression with compassion. Easy-going with good insights, Monkey helps us to consider our options and intuitively sense outcomes.

Monkey awakens playfulness and encourages curiosity, not only about the world but through self-reflection. Monkey inspires us to reacquaint ourselves with ancient wisdom as we explore the origin of our humanity.

MONKEY SAYS

We feel we inspire both fear and fascination in humans. We sometimes laugh at the way you "translate" our wisdom, but we align with you, our cousins, in a good-natured way.

The saying "monkey see, monkey do" is a reminder that you can learn a lot from watching—and so discover different ways of doing. The three monkeys who "see no evil, hear no evil, speak no evil" are instrumental in creating harmony in community.

We show humans how you imprison yourselves when you objectify someone—or some species—and make them separate from you. We offer the teaching that life can be fun and lighthearted without being hurtful to others, and that there is wisdom in play.

We encourage humans to open your minds, feel the relation between our kind and yours, and act in ways that do not harm or separate, but join us all.

We are Monkey and we offer our paw in peace.

Raven

Mysterious and intelligent, Raven is a messenger of magic, a creative communicator with open ties to the spirit world. Raven remembers the "old wisdom" from the time when humans and animals spoke a common language.

Ravens are observant and clever, with a raucous repertoire of shrieks and calls. They can mimic the noises of other animals. The use of sound to alter awareness is part of Raven's teaching, especially as a means of awakening intuition or shifting realities.

Raven helps us to find our inner voice by remembering our core stories—the ones that tell us who we are. Raven brings clarity and understanding to communication through sharing at deeper levels.

Raven is often linked to the Void, where the mysteries of creation reside. Raven is a keeper of secrets, an inventive magician who knows how to transform. Raven connects past with future, death with rebirth. Raven leads us through endings to find beginnings and to make fruitful changes in life.

Well known as a shapeshifter, Raven can help us to alter our awareness so we can see through the eyes of another. This not only allows for abundant perspectives but depth as well—suddenly we can empathize, truly understanding a different perspective of life because we have seen it ourselves. Raven is a master guide to deep transformation.

Raven medicine demands courage and responsibility, requiring us to examine all aspects of ourselves. Raven nudges us to glimpse into the dark corners and confront our shadow. But Raven is willing to walk beside us, helping us to illuminate the darkness.

Helpful creator and harbinger of death, Raven reminds us that the world is full of contradictions. Raven inspires introspection, encourages self-knowledge, and helps us to accept paradox as we embrace the mystery of life.

RAVEN SAYS

Our range extends both far and wide, and deep within. We like your phrase "messenger of magic" for this is what we are—messenger birds who fly between the earth and heavens, linking worlds that were once not so far apart. Times have changed.

We use calls to attract your attention, but we also fly inside you, reminding you of things you already know but forgot along the way.

Our message to humans is to breathe deeply and let yourself soar. Wake up and see the magic and mystery all around you!

We love to fly and dive and twirl. We are acrobatic birds. We love to glide and sail on thermals, and we enjoy watching people.

Our teaching is to tap in to your own joy and mystery so that you too become messengers of magic.

Creation & Creativity

Through the magic of creation, everything and all of us come into existence—stars, planets, mountains, rivers, trees, and toads.

Humans have formulated a wide range of creation myths. In various stories we come from the mating of Mother Earth and Father Sky, the hatching of a giant egg, or the divine breath of a supreme creator. With creation comes the spark, the word, the light, the song—the Big Bang of life unfurling.

Before creation there is nothing—the great void, a vast expanse, primal chaos, the abyss of nothingness. And from that no-thing, some-thing is born.

That's when things start to get creative. From out of the formless comes diversity of form—light and dark; the heavens and the earth; sky, land, and water; rocks and plants; and animals, too.

Creation produces reality and creativity rearranges it. We creatures of earth are incredibly creative, evolving tails and wings, claws and tentacles, gills and fingers, and brains. And that's just the beginning. We radiate the creative impulse simply by being.

For humans, creativity often involves being resourceful, drawing upon what we know and have. Using our imagination, we conceive ideas, devise inventions, design houses, write novels and plays, develop tasty recipes for leftovers, and formulate secret plans.

Creatively inspired, we invent and innovate. The muses whisper in our ears, the gods smile upon us, and everything seems to fall in place. The energy of creativity is often lush, flourishing, wild, and fecund. But there is calm creativity, too—serenely focused, composed, a quiet blooming that flows.

Creativity opens our eyes to fresh ways of seeing, our mind to new avenues of thought, our body to different modes of sensing, and our being to a deepening and widening of experience.

Profound creativity is accompanied by elation. We feel the creative spirit moving inside us and we are in tune, in groove, in ecstasy with all creation. We can't help but smile, for the creative song of life is singing brightly through our soul.

ANIMAL TEACHERS OF CREATION & CREATIVITY

CAT ~ *Intuitive and highly sensitive, Cat helps to fine-tune our creative abilities by teaching precision, elegance, and clarity.*

EAGLE ~ *Keen sight, focus, and the inspired power of flight enable Eagle to help us rise above distractions, discern what we need to create, and take responsibility.*

OCTOPUS ~ *Curious, intelligent, and adaptable, octopuses reveal their creative nature by thinking and feeling outside the box. Octopus highlights the fluid, graceful dimension of creativity.*

PIG ~ *Pig displays compassion and intelligence, helping us to root below the surface to our inner depths, accept ourselves, and discover the fun-loving, creative being within.*

ROBIN ~ *Through the power of song, Robin brings the inspiration of renewal and growth. With Robin's help, we cheer up, get going, and express ourselves in uniquely creative ways.*

Cat

Sensuous and sagacious, cats are free spirits living life on their terms. Long associated with magic and psychic abilities, cats slink through secret passageways, sure-footedly padding through the mysteries of existence. Intuitive, canny, and intelligent, Cat has superb instincts and can assist us in sensory fine-tuning and inter-world travel.

Cats sometimes stare into space or play with invisible friends. That's because Cat has a rich inner world and knows how to peer into other realms. Cat also sees things in our world that we do not.

Cat teaches the use of clarity and cunning. Energized by darkness, at home in the night, Cat deftly navigates through unfamiliar territory, and so is a superb guide through our fears of the shadow world. With acute hearing and excellent vision, Cat offers sharp perception, discernment, and insight.

Cats know how to relax but can be focused and determined as well. Remaining still for long periods, cats watch quietly, furtively, and then—pounce! Agile in both body and mind, Cat inspires us to get out of our rut. Cat arouses awe and wonder, offers a surge of creative vision, and awakens us to magic.

Some cultures honor and venerate cats, while others fear them as dark, supernatural beings. Cat has represented fertility and childbirth; served as protector, guardian, and familiar; and symbolized good luck and fortune. No matter what humans believe, however, Cat holds its own.

Cats can neutralize negative feelings and realign energy fields. As healers, cats work discreetly, sitting nearby, allowing us to pet them, purring to quicken the healing of bones. Cat knows how to restore inner balance and peace.

Resourceful, strong, and fearless, Cat boosts confidence and courage, challenging us to be bold—and helping us to land on our feet. Cat encourages independence, creative thought, and new adventures. Cat is self-assured and encourages us to be the same.

CAT SAYS

Look into our eyes. We live the creative impulse. For us, all is alive with energy. We feel the creative spirit move through us as we leap and run, as we pounce and play, as we sleep and as we dream. We are filled with creativity and this thrills us to the core.

We hold a place in our heart for humans, for we recall a time when we talked freely. Cats were your guides, your supporters and mentors, your champions and beloved friends. We still align ourselves with people, and we often come to you as furry kittens, playful cats, calm companions, and teachers, too.

Our message to humanity is diverse and we have no intention of spelling it out. Come walk with a cat, come sit with a cat, come see the world through our eyes—then you will begin to understand. And we will welcome you home.

Eagle

Soaring 10,000 feet in the air, swooping at 100 miles per hour, Eagle is a powerful bird of grace and extremes. Greatly admired and often revered, Eagle offers a bridge between earth and sky, a symbol of our connection with Spirit.

Eagle enhances intuition and illuminates intelligence with spiritual knowledge. So we open our inner sight, connect with spirit guides and teachers, and begin to perceive the greater landscape of our being. Eagle has strong medicine.

Although eagles have powerful wings and sturdy bodies, their strength has more to do with precision than size. Eagle energy is sharp, swift, focused, determined. We can't fool Eagle—which is why it is often associated with high ideals of freedom and justice.

Eagles have superb vision—eight times more powerful than human eyesight—and can detect prey from miles away. Whether surveying from great heights or zooming in with sharpened clarity, eagles perceive the overall picture. Eagle urges us to let go of small-minded, limited views, inspiring us to rise above them, observe new vistas, and welcome the unknown.

Gliding, hovering, sailing on air currents, eagles ride the wind. Eagle reveals how to harness energy, open up to the power of nature, and allow Spirit to flow through us. With Eagle, our thought is quicker, vision clearer, actions stronger and more effective. Eagle asks us to be brave and take responsibility for our personal power. But Eagle also urges us to experiment, to journey to the far reaches of our imagination in creating what we need to create.

While mating, eagles soar high in the sky, then loop and plummet, locking talons, rolling as one, spiraling downward with great speed and finesse. Eagle unleashes our boldest desires, showing us how to be intimately involved with the spirit of creativity.

EAGLE SAYS

We allow certain students to fly with us, to see through our eyes, and thus understand why Eagle is the one who carries messages to the sun and sky. We work in traditional ways. We appreciate a bit of formality.

We are not reckless but we love to feel our power in the air. We direct our focus to the mysteries of creation. Our medicine is not easy. We hold a truth that not all humans are ready to hear. Our perception penetrates to the core of life.

Our teaching is a way of seeing. For us, inner vision is more a feeling than an action. We feel Spirit flowing through us and that is how we see. If you soar with us, you may feel it suffusing all your cells and soul. It is an experience we long to share.

Octopus

Eight long, suckered tentacles help to make Octopus mysterious and versatile—that and having no shell, no spine, and no bones. Octopuses squeeze in and out of openings smaller than their body diameter. Intelligent and curious, they possess a good memory, can reason and strategize, and are great problem-solvers. Octopus reveals how to loosen up, adapt, be flexible and creative with both body and mind in exploring new places, ideas, and situations.

Experts at camouflage, octopuses have an amazing—and very quick—ability to shift the color, pattern, and texture of their skin, and sometimes seem to vanish. Octopuses are also talented escape artists, squirting black ink to confuse predators and hide their trail. This creative use of color to distract, disorient, and disappear connects Octopus with magic and illusion. Octopus reminds us that things are not always as they seem.

Generally solitary and nocturnal, octopuses can travel far but mostly live on the bottom of the ocean. Octopus reveals how to stay grounded in the depths of our emotional sea. Adrift in shifting currents, at home with fluidity and intuition, Octopus knows how to ride emotion with flexibility and ease.

As ancient creatures, octopuses hold wisdom and memory of esoteric knowledge. Their eight limbs symbolize wholeness, balance, and the coherence of order. Unfurled, the tentacles are nimble, supple, and graceful in movement. Their spiral imagery suggests the universe expanding, creation unfolding, consciousness opening wide.

Octopus medicine may initially be difficult to access. We open up to Octopus by letting go, being fluid, and slipping into the deeper realms. Octopus offers profound teaching, with sensitivity and depth, encouraging us to be curious, to see more and feel more, and to expand ourselves through knowledge, experience, and creative expression.

ROBIN SAYS

We like to arise with the day, hop around grassy lands, and pluck what we need from the earth—worms, bugs, tiny crawling creatures. Yum! Our song is about getting started—taking what you need from the earth and eating it, nourishing yourself so that you can follow your creative dreams.

We build our nests and hatch our young, and we love to sing. So, we offer that teaching as well—how to use your voice, which is your creative spirit, and sing your song to the world.

We are little birds that like to cheer you up and cheer you on. We help to make the world seem less burdensome, and life to progress more smoothly. Once you hear our call and take it to heart, your ideas will flow with ease and joy.

We sing when you are sad to make you happy, and we sing when you are happy to make you glad to be alive.

Dreaming

BEAR ~ DRAGONFLY ~ GROUNDHOG ~ LIZARD ~ SEAL

Eyes closed, body relaxed, we drift away into the darkness of sleep, and suddenly—we awaken in our dreams. Reality is different here, infused with the spirit of transformation. Performing impossible feats, we lift our arms and fly through the air.

Dreaming is a magic that can excite, frighten, awaken, and arouse. Dreams are gateways to distant lands, portals to other dimensions, windows into the past or future. Since ancient times we have been fascinated by our dreams, deeming them oracles, whispers from the gods. We have created special beds, chambers, even temples, to induce dreams, so we can honor and learn from them.

Dreams inspire, encourage, enlighten, and entertain. They predict the future, stimulate ideas, spark solutions, illuminate the hidden, and project dramas within the theatre of our mind. By means of clever hints and clues, dreams offer warnings, advice, healing visions, and prescriptions for our wellbeing.

Dreams are fertile meeting grounds, facilitating a deepening relationship between self and soul. We may encounter ancestors, spirits, wild animals, beloved pets, lost inner selves, and all manner of dream characters. We learn another language, another way of being. Some dreams are frightening, though, and show us things we don't want to see. It requires trust to go the distance with our dreams.

We don't often question where we are in dreams, or what we are doing. We are plunged into situations that feel genuine and real. Then we awaken to everyday reality—or perhaps another type of dreaming? When we are lucid in our dreams, we are awake, aware that we are dreaming. Sometimes while awake, we sense that life is but a dream. Perhaps the dreamworld is just as real as waking reality, or even more so.

Our dreams can amaze us, thrill us, cause our limbs to flail and heart to pound. At the end of the day, the dream shines—astute, perceptive, wise. Dreams have stories to tell, questions to ask. Dreaming is a mystery, a grand adventure, a celebration, a profound invitation to know ourselves in deeper ways.

ANIMAL TEACHERS OF DREAMING

BEAR ~ *Powerful dreamer and expert guide to introspection, Bear encourages us to explore the unknown and find our own answers in the calm silence of our inner dream cave.*

DRAGONFLY ~ *Combining the beauty of light and the power of flight, Dragonfly helps us to recall delicate dreams, and travel easily through dreamtime.*

GROUNDHOG ~ *Weighty, self-assured, balanced, Groundhog is a grounder, helping us to stay in our body even as we tunnel through the distant reaches of dreamworld.*

LIZARD ~ *Long known for its ability to help shamans and dreamers to connect with other realms of consciousness, Lizard reminds us to respect our dreams and to move through illusions to find wisdom within.*

SEAL ~ *Smart and playful, Seal guides us to the deep sea of self and helps us to retrieve our deepest dreams. Sometimes awakening us inside our dreams, Seal is also a helpful guide to lucid dreaming.*

Bear

From the very beginning, humans sensed a kinship with Bear. Bears can stand upright, are curious and intelligent, protective of their young and, without their skins, look remarkably human. Many ancient cultures honored and worshipped Bear. In its great, hearty spirit we recognized a teacher and ally. Symbol of the creative unconscious, Bear is a powerful dreamtime advisor.

Most bears slow down and sleep through much of the winter. They are not true hibernators, but instinctively know when to retire and be alone with their dormant energies. Pondering deeply in the dark cover of cave or den, they immerse themselves in dreamtime. Females may give birth while sleeping. Dreaming with their cubs, they share collective bear wisdom, personal life experience, and instructive previews of life outside the den.

Bear's determined focus and good-natured spirit of inquiry enables it to root out hidden truths, prompting us to explore the unknown and seek adventure in our dreams. Sometimes serious, often humorous, Bear is a superb guide and protective travel companion. Bear often shows up in dreams to encourage self-reflection and nudge us toward deeper meanings.

Bear emphasizes independence and introspection, urging us to slow down and look inside ourselves when we need help. Bear knows that in the calm silence of our deepest being, we can see and hear clearly. Alert and aware in the dreamworld, we will find our answers.

In spring, bears awaken, hungry for new opportunities, companionship, and food. Bear links dreams with awakening, bringing together the feminine yin of introspection with the masculine yang of action. Bear reminds us to maintain balance in the natural rhythms of life. From the dark, nurturing, fertile cave of dreams, we emerge into the sunlight, assimilating our experiences and sharing our discoveries with the world. Bear cheers us on.

GROUNDHOG SAYS

Deep sleep and extended journeys of consciousness are our forte. We travel with distinction, for we have learned the ins and outs of dreamtime voyaging. With us, you get a first-class ticket to deep adventure.

Our teaching is not for everyone, but our medicine is self-regulating. You will absorb only as much as you can handle. We have worked with some advanced human students and very much enjoy this cooperation. As the earth changes, you may need more of our medicine. We connect with dense earth energies that originate deep within and rise to the surface in subtle ways. Yet, in their depth there is much power and creative energy.

We also work in gentle ways. We can help you to burrow and form your own pathways to the dreamworld. The more you travel them, the clearer they will be. That is an early teaching from us, the groundhogs of planet earth.

Lizard

Roaming the earth for over 200 million years, lizards have evolved into 5,000 different forms. Lizards can glide through the air, race across water, walk on ceilings, change the color of their skin, and shed their tail and grow a new one. Amazingly adaptable, Lizard is watchful and perceptive, an ancient survivor who is well acquainted with the dreamtime.

Long known for its ability to help dreamers connect with other realms of consciousness, Lizard is a firm yet patient teacher. Lizard urges us to remember and respect our dreams, and knows the power of using dreams to contemplate different futures and imagine possible outcomes. At home in the dreamworld, Lizard reveals how to preview reality before it is real.

Lizards are cold blooded and require sunlight to warm themselves. Some lizards turn brilliant colors in the sunshine, while others are naturally bright with jewel-like designs or detailed patterns. Lizard dreaming is similarly vivid and bold, sometimes psychedelic in imagery. With Lizard, we learn to slow down, soak in the sun, and observe the radiance of life. Lizard prompts us to pay attention to details and recurring patterns—valuable clues—in our dreams.

With excellent hearing and eyesight, Lizard is also highly attuned to movement and vibration. Extremely sensitive in so many areas, Lizard is an expert at subtle perceptions. Lizard helps us to awaken and to fine tune our inner senses so that we may recognize hidden symbols and messages in our dreams.

Often considered an advanced dream teacher, Lizard guides us to higher forms of knowledge. Lizard reminds us that dreams reveal our hidden fears and desires, and often show us much more than we may care to know. If accepted as Lizard's student, we will learn about intensifying dreamtime perceptions and bridging them—courageously, patiently—with conscious awareness.

LIZARD SAYS

We are great observers, very familiar with the tunnels that open profound perception. They allow us in to another way of seeing reality—a deep reality that you might consider to be a different reality.

We teach that dreaming is not different from waking but a continuum of experience. Waking, dreaming, sitting, staring into the tunnels of perception—where are "you" within yourself? This is the "reality" you will see.

If we were humans, we would be philosophers. You may laugh but this is Lizard seeing.

To know of deep perception, sit with a lizard in the sun. Slow your breathing, feel the warmth, and allow yourself to soften. Soon you will see an opening in whatever you are looking at. Follow it far enough and you will emerge in a dreamtime. It is not other than you, but an extension of you. That is how we see it.

Seal

LUCID DREAMER ~ FLUID DANCER ~ CONNECTS DEEP SEA AND SELF

The link between humans and seals is very old. Ancient peoples hunted seals and used every part of the animal to survive. Those humans honored and loved the seal, and some believed they were descended from the union of seals and humankind. Others told stories of the magical selkies, who slip out of their sealskins to become human and walk on land. Seal connects us with mystery and the power of our dreams.

Seals spend most of their lives in the ocean but give birth on land. Their eyes are large and round, to focus in both air and water. Like the selkies, seals are of two worlds.

Floating, diving, rolling, twisting, speeding through the sea, seals love to explore and play. With sensual ease, Seal helps us to feel more comfortable in our physical body and inspires fluidity of movement in our dream body.

While seals can be lively and full of fun, Seal's serious side pulls us far down. Seals can stay submerged for an hour and dive to a depth of well over 1,000 feet. This connection with deep water reveals Seal as a wisdom keeper, in touch with oceanic rhythms and currents of the psyche. Seal assists us in remembering our deepest dreams, especially those we have forgotten because they seem too dense or cumbersome to bring to the surface.

Seal awakens inner vision in dreams, and often shows up to remind us that we are dreaming. Gently nudging us awake inside our dreams, Seal can be a supportive guide to lucid dreaming.

Seal inspires curiosity and creativity in the dream state, and encourages us to transport the playfulness and healing visions of dreams into our waking life. Seal helps us to find out who we are, prompting us to dive down, discover the mysteries of our depths, and buoy that knowledge to conscious awareness.

DOG SAYS

Our healing is the joy of being, of partnership and friendliness, of simple things—walking, running, sniffing, chasing, and playing when you want to play.

We have a pact with humans, an agreement from ancient times. We are attuned to you, aligned in the heart-space of love and protection.

We play many roles to help you find your inner Dog. We like to amuse you with our antics and comfort you when you are sad. We sit beside you; we wait with you as you evolve. Our healing is about softening yourself, opening your heart to joy and fun.

With Dog, what you see is what you get. We see clear and true. We encourage you to express the fullness of who you are. We trust you to shine brightly. We are Dog. We know how to play and touch your soul with love. We will be with you to the end.

Frog

Frogs have lived on earth for several hundred million years, and their 5000 species are found almost everywhere. Symbol of good luck, fertility, abundance, and a happy family life, Frog is also linked to human healing. Frog parts were used widely in the ancient world as remedies, and frog secretions and toxins are a potent mystery valued by modern medicine. Recognized as a deep healer, Frog has a strong spirit and holds old magic that speaks of change, cleansing, renewal, and rebirth.

Frogs' eggs hatch into tadpoles, which develop into adults. Frog energy inspires adaptation and smooth transformation between different states of being. Frog helps us to swim through major life transitions and to leap into new situations or the next stage of consciousness. Frog medicine moves fluidly and naturally, yet works deeply. Healing comes through finding balance—both within ourselves and within our world.

Frogs are sensitive and they easily absorb pollutants through their skin. Frog populations are thus good indicators of our planet's environmental health. Some cultures view Frog as a rainmaker that calls forth the healing power of water to cleanse and purify the earth. Frog nudges us to sink into our deeper emotions and use the flowing water of tears to release negativity, blocked energies, and accumulated toxins. Frog refreshes our outlook on life, encouraging us to nourish and renew ourselves by calling forth our inner healer.

Frogs chirp, peep, trill, tap, twang, and croak. Frog urges us to loosen up, express our inner voice, and let our creative nature flow. Frog's appearance often signals a new direction in life, a hint that we may need to change some aspect of ourselves for deep healing to occur.

Frog sings the creation song, reminding us of our watery beginnings and connection with all life. With Frog, we celebrate transformation as we continue to evolve.

FROG SAYS

We live in many different circumstances, in many different places, and always we find ways to adapt. That is one of our healing gifts—to show you how to adapt by having fun in your own way, and with what you do.

We find life to be full of wonder and delight. We are curious about the world. We aren't boxed in. We can jump and swim, leap and sink down into the earth or water. We encourage movement as part of change. That, too, is healing—move your body to loosen up and allow change to happen naturally.

Frogs are excellent mentors. We like to work with children and inspire them to think in new ways. We feel this is an important aspect of healing—to keep yourself fresh and active, chirping with life, always ready to hop into a new situation and see life with big, happy eyes. We are Frog!

Gorilla

Intelligent and wise, with deep, soulful eyes, Gorilla is calm, steady, and quietly reserved. Gorillas have great physical strength but rarely resort to violence. Kind, good-natured, and easy-going, gorillas are accepting, often sharing food and space. Gorilla teaches integrity and honor. Large and powerful, Gorilla has a big heart and reveals dignity through gentleness and peaceful living.

Gorillas enjoy private time but are also sociable with family and community. Most gorillas live in troops led by a dominant male who has learned to balance authority with respect for others. Firm yet considerate, Gorilla shows us that by treating others with honesty and decency we will thrive together.

Gorillas are extremely intelligent and use a wide range of sounds and gestures to communicate. They laugh, whimper, cry, bark, hoot, beat their chests, bare their teeth, and shake tree branches. Gorillas have sensitive fingers—similar in appearance to our own—and often speak with their hands. They are especially attuned to subtle movements and looks, prompting us to notice nuance, trust our feelings and perceptions, and be gentle when conversing with others.

Gorillas are loyal and protective, sharing responsibility in caring for both young and old. They also listen well. Gorilla teaches us to be fully present and to listen attentively. Profound healing can occur both when we listen deeply and when we feel that we are truly heard. Gorilla prompts us to inhabit the healing space of presence.

We often sense a familiarity with Gorilla—and, indeed, we are closely related. Gorilla reveals nobility, although not as pride or through boasting. Gorilla recognizes the honorable being within, reminding us that we are much more than appearances. Gorilla encourages us to find and express our deep self, especially in relationship with others and our planet. This is how we heal.

Fox says

Much of our work with humans involves opening up your senses, helping you to observe life more keenly, and to experience the world more fully. To those who are patient and alert, we reveal passageways to different dimensions. We can also help you to find such openings within yourself. We are guides to a special form of integration. But we can only lead you so far.

We experience deep peace through observing life, although we also know when to participate with gusto and delight! We value the art of timing and moving with precision. We find pleasure in knowing when to freeze and when to leap, sliding between moments to catch prey or escape predators.

We are foxy—skilled, finely tuned, agile, sly. If you need help in seeing more clearly, moving more deftly, or finding the way you fit into the world, come sit with a fox. We observe the world with alert integrity.

Hippopotamus

Often immersed in water, hippopotamuses are at home in the fluid world of emotions, dreams, and creativity. Their eyes, ears, and nostrils open high on their head, allowing them to be aware of what's going on above the surface even while they are almost fully submerged. Hippo reveals how to integrate thoughts and feelings, creative insights and action. With Hippo, we learn to glide safely through our emotional depths while maintaining presence and perspective in daily life.

During the day, hippopotamuses avoid sunburn and overheating by sinking low in the water. In the evening, they leave the river individually to dine on grasses. To and from favorite grazing grounds, their heavy bodies and stubby legs create well-worn paths, which other animals follow during the day. Hippo plows the way for others, helping us to find the path of least resistance. Hippo links water to land, encouraging us to ground our dreams with substance and practicality.

Despite their size, hippos are agile and fast. They can also turn quickly—physically and emotionally. Hippos possess joyful and aggressive sides, a mercurial temperament manifest in mobility. Hippo tolerates only the very well-behaved, demanding that we respect others and ourselves. Territorial in water, hippopotamuses remind us to recognize what we feel and where we belong.

Hippos grunt and bellow, and have a special call that penetrates air and water simultaneously. Hippo communicates between worlds, and can foster conversation with the spirit realm or facilitate lucid dreaming, leading us to integrate spiritual insights and dreams with conscious awareness.

Rotund and voluminous, Hippo helps us to recognize, accept, and welcome all aspects of our character, and to integrate them into a larger, fuller, more well-rounded expression of our true selves.

HIPPO SAYS

We are stable, solid. We draw knowledge and a sense of camaraderie from water, which amplifies feelings and sensations. We know what others are doing because we feel it through our bodies. In water, we feel each other and we know.

We know of humans and your actions throughout the world—all this is held in water. Energy—thoughts, feelings, actions—moves across the earth and is absorbed by land, condensed in water. This is how we know what is happening in the world. You cannot lie to earth or water ... everything comes through.

If you learn to sink and listen, to feel and open, you will know this, too. We are at peace with ourselves and do not often interact with others. We speak to quiet souls who are happy being alone even when around others. That is Hippo knowledge, a special kind of tone.

Peacock

Well known for their brilliant blue-green coloring, crown-like crest, and regal tail display, peacocks are associated with nobility, guidance, and protection. In ancient times, peacocks were watchful guardians of royalty, and represented the immortal soul, the sun, and spiritual awakening.

Peacocks are playful and pursue pleasure. With their loud calls and proud displays, they revel in life. However, peacocks are also birds of habit. They like to feed in the same place, drink at the same watering hole, and roost in trees they know. Peacock persuades us to have fun and enjoy ourselves, but also to relish the comforts of home.

Generous and insightful, Peacock encourages us to be at home with ourselves. Peacock teaches wholeness, urging us to shift from what we think is wrong or missing in our life and, instead, appreciate what we see before us. Inspiring us to embrace all aspects of ourselves, especially those we judge ugly or unlovable, Peacock helps us to rediscover our inner beauty.

Confident, dignified, Peacock knows that true beauty comes from within—although there's nothing wrong with expressing it outwardly. Peacock boosts our self-esteem, cheering us to shine boldly, and to show our regal self in full, glorious color.

Peacocks display their trains to impress peahens. In the sunlight, peacock feathers shimmer with iridescence, a touch of magic. Peacock feathers help to dissipate negative energies and build strong, solid auras with healthy energy fields. The "eyes" of the feathers represent wisdom, spiritual insight, and clarity of vision. Peacock helps us to see into the past and future, and integrate our discoveries with the present.

Peacocks have a variety of loud calls, some eerie, some raucous, some with a hint of laughter. Peacock reminds us to loosen up, behave naturally, and be happy with our own personality. Peacock celebrates wholeness and reminds us to do the same.

PEACOCK SAYS

We like pageantry and show. We (males) express ourselves and we (females) appreciate the show. This works well for us. We integrate "display" and "view." We put on a spectacle to see ourselves—as do you. Many humans boast, call for attention, and exhibit colorful splendor. Others prefer to watch, to be bedazzled by colors, action, and sound. It works well, don't you think? For us, that is a key aspect of integration.

We help everyone to find their big display inside. When you shine your inner colors, others are inspired. And when you see the extravaganzas of others, you may care to shimmer your ideas as well. Everyone wins!

We are all viewers and displayers, watchers and revealers. We look noble and regal because we are. Proud as a peacock is a phrase of empowerment. We think we wear it well. We hope you do, too.

Swan

ELEGANCE ~ DISCERNMENT ~ GRACE ~ BEAUTY ~ STRENGTH

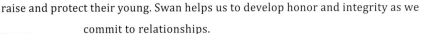

Muse to poets, artists, and musicians, symbol of love and spirit, Swan enchants the world with beauty and grace. In ancient legends, humans transform into swans when moving between realms, or swans sing so bewitchingly they put people to sleep. Swan's teaching is powerful—often deceptively so.

With their elegant, curved necks, bright white feathers, and smooth, gliding movements, swans seem ethereal and delicate. Actually, they are quite hardy and strong. Swans migrate long distances and will break the bones of intruders during nesting time. Swan brings our hidden strengths to light, reminding us that appearances can be misleading.

Swan's strong spirit requires respect. Associated with courtship and fidelity, swans usually mate for life. They travel in pairs—an integration of male and female, a partnership of devotion. Both parents raise and protect their young. Swan helps us to develop honor and integrity as we commit to relationships.

As waterbirds, swans paddle through the fluidity of feelings, dreams, and creativity. They feed by dipping their heads in and out of water, reminding us to approach inner work gently, to integrate emotional insights carefully and attentively.

As migrators and birds of the air, swans fly great distances at high altitudes. Swan links our inner world with the airy, spiritual nature of flight. Swan opens us to altered states of consciousness and visions of the future, encouraging us to spread our wings and gather knowledge.

Gliding through water, walking on land, soaring through air, Swan integrates different worlds and realities. Swan stimulates us to balance our consciousness—whether dipping below the surface of our emotions, flying high, or grounding ourselves on earth. Swan helps us to integrate with discernment, discovering our own dignity, strength, and elegance.

SWAN SAYS

We encompass many worlds. We encounter many different situations, lands, and environments. There are many faces to Swan! Yet always we are centered in our core being.

We hold a strong center of inner knowing. And joy! We embrace new situations. We devote ourselves to the task at hand. When nesting, we give it our all. When raising our young, we focus our vision and love. When moving between lands, we thrill to the air as we sail through clouds. In the water, we carry ourselves with pride.

Our teaching is about moving seamlessly, adapting to any moment with grace. That comes from the center inside ourselves. Do you see? That is Swan's teaching—integrating every moment, every situation, with the full presence of your own self. That is how you develop a strong center. That is how you reveal beauty in the world.

Zebra

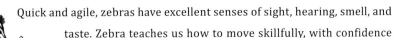

One of the oldest members of the horse family, Zebra is easily recognized by its distinctive black and white stripes. Each zebra's pattern is unique, like a human fingerprint, marking its individuality within the herd.

A lone zebra in the savannah is very conspicuous and thus vulnerable to predators. But in a group, all those stripes confuse predators, making the herd look like one huge animal, too large to attack. Zebra's clever form of camouflage reminds us that what we think we see isn't always what is there.

Zebra teaches the benefit of belonging to a group without losing our individuality. As social animals, zebras equally reveal the importance of honoring family and community. Zebra encourages us to share our special talents—and celebrate the talents of others. With Zebra, we learn to integrate group consciousness while maintaining our sense of self.

Zebra helps us to acknowledge and accept opposing viewpoints, and move on. Under Zebra's tutelage, we realize that things are not simply black or white, but rather both black and white. Zebra medicine works to unblock stubborn patterns of "right" and "wrong", judgments and prejudice. Zebra reminds us that we are all planetary citizens with distinct and important roles to play.

Quick and agile, zebras have excellent senses of sight, hearing, smell, and taste. Zebra teaches us how to move skillfully, with confidence and clarity, and remain centered even in the midst of confusion.

In learning to perceive beyond illusion, we discover how to integrate both light and dark energies within ourselves, and within our world. When Zebra nuzzles near, hidden knowledge may soon be revealed.

ZEBRA SAYS

We evoke compassion out of confusion, tranquility from discord. Our teaching for humanity is about learning to accept all parts of yourself—dark and light. We work to harmonize that which seems to be at cross-purposes. Our distinctive coloring is a reminder that black and white viewpoints are reflections of what is seen and unseen.

Just as alternating stripes flow along our body contours and make our kind—and each within our kind—unique, we reveal the beauty of contrast. We speak of the value of each stripe, each path, each individual as an essential part of the whole.

We offer the healing reminder that by opening your heart, you may come to know a deeper sense of belonging. All individuals are important and contribute in different ways. Thus we create wholeness upon our planet. This is the beauty of our healing.

Intuition

CHICKEN ~ JAGUAR ~ LLAMA ~ MANTIS ~ RHINOCEROS

Properly defined as knowledge gained without conscious reasoning or the use of our five senses, intuition is basically our sixth sense, direct perception. Difficult to prove and hard for some to discern, intuition can seem mysterious, an enigmatic way of knowing.

It can be an instinctive awareness or a physical sensation. We may feel something in our gut, have butterflies in our stomach, or just know in our bones. Intuition can also be mental sensing—a flash of knowing, a sudden clarity, a deep-down certainty, a revelatory vision. Deep intuition is immediate and undeniable.

Intuition nudges us to sense what's going on beneath the surface, so we often know exactly what it is, despite what people say or do.

Intuition is an opening. The doors of perception fling open wide and we can move through space and time. Sensing deeper, following the flow of feelings, riding the inspiration of insight and inner vision, we open ourselves to larger frameworks of reality.

To intuit means to look inside, and sometimes we may stumble unexpectedly into the "is-ness" of existence. We may be looking at a rose, a bird, a blade of grass and suddenly we know the spirit within.

Intuition helps us to be more open-minded, more welcoming of both what is and what might come. We intuitively sense patterns, hints, and clues. The world is alive and vibrant, full of meaning, signs, and symbols. We recognize the secrets that have been present all along.

Some feel that as intuition develops, our consciousness evolves. Our awareness expands and also deepens. Sometimes all our senses seem heightened, as if our sixth sense is a booster, adding depth and flavor, texture and fullness to the experience of sensory knowing.

With keen intuition, we know when to act and what to do. Freed from the clutter of thought, we open to clarity, knowing what is. In flow with all life, we sense our path within the larger scheme.

ANIMAL TEACHERS OF INTUITION

CHICKEN ~ *Proud and purposeful, Chicken helps us to find our truth, focus our vision, develop sensitivity, open our empathic channels to others, and remain grounded.*

JAGUAR ~ *Long known for its association with inner-world journeys, Jaguar helps us to move in the shadows. Focused and discerning, Jaguar refines intuition and cultivates confidence in our abilities.*

LLAMA ~ *Both grounders and expanders, llamas lighten our load when we are traveling, and put us in touch with the finer frequencies of spirit. Llama regulates energies, helping us to hum our way to enlightenment.*

MANTIS ~ *Teacher, warrior, master of mindful movement, Mantis reveals the secret of stillness, and helps us to fine tune our intuition with meticulous precision.*

RHINOCEROS ~ *Thick-skinned, yet highly sensitive, Rhinoceros is ancient and wise. Rhino helps us to stay balanced and trust our instincts as we open ourselves to far-ranging expanses of awareness.*

Chicken

NOBLE SPIRIT ~ CREATIVE TEACHER ~ UNCOVERS TRUTH ~ AWAKENS THE WORLD

They can't fly high or any great distance, so chickens are more oriented to land than sky. Inquisitive and observant, attuned to small areas of ground, chickens hold a deep, centered, and very practical wisdom. Chicken uncovers truth and awakens intuition, prodding us to listen to our inner voice and to trust hunches.

With purposeful determination, chickens use their toes to scratch the ground and unearth food, searching until they find what they want. Chicken has a focused ability to expose truth that lies hidden just beneath the surface.

Chickens notice changes in their environment. Living so close to the ground enables them to attune to the soil, absorbing energy from the earth. Chicken is empathic and can help fine tune our intuition, making us more aware of the thoughts and feelings of others. However, Chicken cautions us to avoid oversensitivity by remaining grounded, centered in our body, connected to the land.

Proud and noble, chickens are intelligent and self-reflective. When they sense danger, they will protect their personal space. Chicken's strong spirit encourages us to learn and to take in new ideas, to develop proficiency in all areas of life, and to help others through teaching and offering ideas. Chicken understands the power of sharing knowledge.

There are many varieties of chickens, with widely different colors, patterns, and feather displays. Considered a sacred bird and a channel to the spirit world, chickens are sometimes used in sacrifice. Chicken connects us to earth and the heavens, to buried secrets and spirit visions. Chicken represents creativity and fertility.

Unique and independent, even when living in groups, chickens behave naturally as individuals. Just as a rooster crows loud and bold and clear, Chicken helps us to wake up and announce ourselves to the world.

CHICKEN SAYS

We think of ourselves as unconventional and a lot of fun. True, we know how to hunker down, lay eggs, and nurture our young, but we possess a wild side as well.

We help humans in many ways—not just for meat and eggs. We peck away at problems in the world. We delight you with our feathers, colors, and dances.

Our spirit is untamed, even though you think you have tamed us. We know how to play a role. We are Chicken—elaborate, fanciful, talented.

We are often used in ceremony and ritual—that is a clue to our power. We help you to tap into your spiritual presence.

We see details with clarity and sharp inner vision. When you are confused, we can help direct your sight. We sometimes act things out so you can see them more clearly. We help you to know yourselves better.

Jaguar

SECRETIVE ~ ELUSIVE ~ INSTILLS CONFIDENCE ~ WORKS IN THE DARK

Ancient and mysterious, Jaguar has long been associated with royalty, rulers, shamans, and warriors. Worshipped by the Mayans, Aztecs, and Incas, Jaguar was a fierce god of fertility and sacrifice, both revered and feared for its power. Shapeshifter and master guide to astral-realm journeys, Jaguar facilitates between-world travel, and opens communication between the living and the dead. As a spiritual guide and protector, Jaguar prompts us to focus and refine our intuition.

At home in the night, Jaguar leads us deep into the dark. Peering into other dimensions, Jaguar hears the thoughts of other animals and beings, and helps us to do the same. Jaguar urges us to trust our inner perceptions, to understand that they are real—invitations to different modes of experience. Silent, capable, and discerning, Jaguar sees patterns and pathways in chaos. Jaguar encourages us to stay directed, true to ourselves and the power of our insights.

Bold and fearless, Jaguar helps us to see in the dark as we traverse dreams, shadow worlds, and unfamiliar territory. Jaguar's intensity and focus activates psychic perceptions, guiding us to release fears and gain confidence as we use our power.

Jaguars are sturdy and swift, agile climbers who follow their prey with steadfast determination. Prowling patiently, stalking silently, jaguars wait for just the right moment to pounce. Their powerful jaws snap spines and pierce skulls with a single bite. Jaguars also like to swim, unusual for cats, and can help as we move through emotional waters.

As a solitary hunter, Jaguar reminds us that some pursuits are best done alone. Jaguar persuades us to follow inner guidance rather than be influenced by others. Prodding us to focus on what really matters, Jaguar urges us to gather courage and face our spiritual challenges well prepared. Jaguar helps us to reclaim our power.

JAGUAR SAYS

Our vision is focused. We see not only in the dark but in the darkness of your soul. We are soul walkers and the intensity of our medicine is deep.

We usually work first as companion and guide. We teach but also watch—carefully. We discern when a student is ready. We tend to work with humans who already have some training, or an intense desire to shadow walk.

Our teaching is not verbal or mental, but feeling-based. We teach you to move from center—and to know center in every cell of your body. This is not something most humans are familiar with. In the astral realm, your body is more sensitive and you can feel centered presence with all your being. That is the focus we offer.

If you are drawn to us, come near to watch. When you are ready, we will invite you in.

Llama

Insightful, intelligent, and highly intuitive, llamas are natural healers and balancers. Most people feel good near llamas. That's because llamas hold and share high frequencies of energy. Llama stimulates our awareness of spiritual dimensions within everyday reality, helping us to expand in practical ways and making us more sensitive as human beings. Llama energy liberates!

Llamas work in subtle ways, often beneath our conscious recognition, rebalancing and realigning discordant energy patterns. Llamas assist psychic growth, nudging us to assimilate higher energies, ground them in our body, and express them creatively in unique ways.

Gregarious, gentle, and caring, llamas live in herds, valuing each member's individual contributions. Linked by herd consciousness, llamas stay in close contact by sharing intuitive perceptions. Llama teaches balance of self and group, and keeps telepathic lines open and flowing smoothly.

Llamas often hum to communicate. Different hums have different meanings, and the humming tone reveals much about Llama medicine. Llama is a gatekeeper, linking star energies to earth. Llama can help us to stay centered and grounded as we perceive subtle frequencies and expand in otherworldly dimensions.

Sure-footed and strong, llamas transport cargo along high tracks in mountainous areas. Llama helps us to maneuver through difficult, steep terrain, and to find secure footing. Llama guides us to the right path. Llama also offers emotional grounding, reminding us to breathe deeply and take things slowly when stressed with heavy loads. With Llama, we learn to balance our actions.

Curious and independent, Llama helps us to travel lightly across space and time, prompting us to rely upon our intuition, clearly seeing what is and what will be.

Llama says

We regulate energy, spirit, and light. Our place is high in the mountains because that is where reception is best. We attune energies to earth, and can help you to do the same.

We like to hum—and we know how humming in the world can assist you. To hum is to vibrate, to make a sound frequency that is also a vehicle. Your hum is your personal energetic tone—what keeps you alive and gives you your uniqueness. Each tone is individual, yet all are joined. You could say we are harmonizers, helping to attune frequencies and hums within the world.

If you want to relax and heal, hum! If you want to see more clearly, hum! Humming is not the answer, but a beginning. By humming, you become more aware of so much within yourself. You can travel without moving. We bow our heads and hum to you.

Mantis

Sacred symbol, ancient teacher, Mantis is a master of adaptability and camouflage. The word Mantis comes from the Greek, meaning prophet or seer. Mantises have triangular faces and huge eyes, and can swivel their heads—unusual for insects—and look around. For Mantis, intuition means foresight, timing, and precision.

There are 2,000 forms of Mantis, color coded to match their environments—bright fern green, lichen orange, pebbly blue, flower-stamen pink, even the hue and texture of a dead leaf. Mantises hunt by ambush, waiting, still and silent, blending into the background, watching, listening, sensing the fullness of a situation before they strike. Then, in a flash—one quick bite to the head—it's over. Thus a praying mantis becomes a preying mantis.

Mantis reveals how to use stillness as a springboard to expanded consciousness. With a calm body and mind, we are able to awaken inner perceptions, remaining attentive in stillness. Subtle channels of energy are revealed. We sense at deeper levels, discovering solutions to problems, discerning the future. Mantis is a helpful guide to contemplation and dreams.

Although an expert at patience, a strong, active, warrior energy flows through Mantis as well. At the critical moment, Mantis springs into action—swift and elegant, simple and clear. Mantis is a master at mindful motion, an inspiration to martial arts practitioners. Moving with Mantis, we feel fully alive, in the zone, balanced in mind and body.

Mantis is also a trickster and dreamer. In African bushman lore, Mantis gets into trouble but dreams a solution. Mantis reveals how to access higher realms of consciousness, manipulate time, and travel to secret worlds. Mantis helps us to discover our power through the mystery of stillness, and to sense the dream that is dreaming us.

MANTIS SAYS

We are aware of much in the world. We are a different order, privy to different secrets and ways of perceiving and interacting with reality. Thus, our version of the world may seem entirely alien to you.

One of our teachings regards doorways between worlds, portals that lead in and out of time. This is the "magic" many masters of movement once sought from us.

If you follow our motions and move into our reality, you may experience quite an awakening! We are very small compared to you, yet in our world, we are immense. We can be huge or so small we are invisible. That is another teaching we hold.

Our teaching is not for everyone, but on general levels we can help you to think quicker, move faster, and be clearer in your actions. We nod our heads to you. Thank you for taking time to listen.

Rhinoceros

Strong, solid, stable, and resilient, rhinoceroses have lived on earth for 60 million years. Rhinoceros knows how to be patient and persevere. In touch with ancient wisdom, Rhino uncovers buried knowledge and memories of past lives. Generally solitary, and comfortable being alone, rhinoceroses help us to sink into solitude, enjoy our own company, and commune with our deeper self. Indeed, Rhino's teaching is "know thyself."

Rhinos have poor eyesight but heightened senses of hearing and smell. Roaming open spaces, inhaling the rich, grassy air, they savor scent, which triggers memories. Wallowing in cool, muddy waters, they embrace earth energies to refresh and heal. Rhino guides us to relish sensory experience and use our instincts to know ourselves better.

Although rhinos are highly sensitive, their thick, strong skin provides a protective armor. Rhino prods us to let go of outer distractions while shielding us from oversensitivity and too much external influence. Thoughtful and wise, Rhino teaches us to trust intuition and accept the sage advice of our inner counsel. Rhino helps us to find balance and solidity within. With Rhino, we feel secure, centered, and grounded, even as we open to vast expanses of awareness.

Although rhinos will charge when attacked or frightened, they are usually peaceful. Rhino teaches us to observe first. If action is needed, Rhino can help us to launch it and follow through.

Rhinoceroses use their horns (African rhinos have two; Asian rhinos have one) to dig, forage, impress a potential mate, intimidate, and defend. Long coveted by humans for status, medicine, or magic, rhino horn symbolizes discernment—especially the ability to see through illusion. Ironically, Rhino teaches that power does not lie outside ourselves—in the horn of another—but within. Rhino encourages us to find true power by seeing inside ourselves.

RHINO SAYS

Once upon a time, we were honored for our wisdom and consulted by the human world.

We spend our days close to the earth and have learned much in our many years. We feel connection with the center of the earth and with the surface, too—trees and grasses, mud and water. We understand the link between surface and depth. That is why we were often called upon to offer our advice.

We are generally happy creatures, travelers, roaming these lands. We feel sad that so many humans don't see our wisdom, wanting only to cut off our horns, as if this can help.

What we want to say to humans is this—calm down, go within, listen deep. We invite you to roam the deep expanse of your soul. Find us there. We are happy to talk, to recall the old days when a human and a rhino could consult in peace.

GROUP 9

Joy

DOLPHIN ~ GOAT ~ GOLDFISH ~ HUMMINGBIRD ~ OTTER

Delight, happiness, glee, bliss, ecstasy, and euphoria—these are the bright-eyed, twinkling faces of joy. Invigorating and enlivening, joy reminds us how much fun it is to be made of flesh and blood, how thrilling to be alive! We feel elation, we bubble over with exuberance and *joie de vivre*. We can't help but lose ourselves in crazy whoops of pleasure. Tingling in the rush of exhilaration, we sparkle brightly. Effervescent, like good champagne, we dance in celebration. Joy is a glorious smile, the whoosh of a waltz, the trill of a mysterious bird.

Sometimes an undervalued emotion, joy shows us who we are. Children and animals feel joy easily, celebrating simple things in nature. We share joy when we play, laugh, and stumble into fun. Seeing the world with wonder and delight, touched by life's magic, we behold the sacred grove of joy.

Joy is surprising—and wise. It can rise quickly or simmer slowly. It can clamor boisterously or linger quietly inside of us, like a forgotten secret we always knew. We can thrill to joy with sudden insight or understanding. Our intellect may be transported with happiness.

We can find joy in moments of beauty and ecstatic raptures of the heart. It may accompany the first breath or the last exhalation, welcoming the possibilities of what is to come or affirming the path of a life well lived. Joy can be contagious, burbling over like a magic stew. We can glory in joy, feel triumph and peaceful happiness, too.

We can't force joy or grasp it tightly. Sometimes shy and elusive, joy disappears when we try to hold on or won't let go. Joy comes without expectations, overflowing, demanding nothing. It can be fleeting, like a well-loved guest who leaves too soon. Joy shimmers in sunlit, dappled leaves.

Spontaneous, mysterious, ever patient, joy waits for us, smiling calmly in our heart.

ANIMAL TEACHERS OF JOY

DOLPHIN ~ *Intelligent, creative, perceptive lover of fun, Dolphin nudges us to be more aware of our real selves. With Dolphin we expand our consciousness and deepen our joy.*

GOAT ~ *Savvy, stable, agile, and sure-footed, Goat inspires us to embrace our curiosity, explore both inner and outer worlds, find our center, and follow our joy.*

GOLDFISH ~ *Symbol of good luck and joy, Goldfish awakens us to happiness, harmony, and the deep, fluid peace of inner calm.*

HUMMINGBIRD ~ *Although small, Hummingbird holds the big teaching of how to open up to magic and wonder. When Hummingbird flies into our heart, we thrill to the joy of being alive.*

OTTER ~ *Naturally curious and friendly, Otter is a skillful teacher of exuberance and play. With Otter, we learn to relax, have fun, and accept the joy that comes our way.*

Dolphin

Playful, friendly, and highly intelligent, Dolphin speaks to us about humanity. Naturally inquisitive and creative, dolphins adapt easily. They devise games, race through the water, ride waves, and leap into the air for sheer joy.

As marine mammals, dolphins must stay awake to surface and breathe. They sleep by resting half their brain at a time. Never fully unconscious, dolphins know that each breath is a choice. Dolphin shows us how to be more aware of ourselves with every breath we take. Dolphins breathe in deeply and release with gusto. Breathing like a dolphin enables us to let go of suppressed emotions and move through our feelings. Dolphin prompts us to let go of our anxieties and enjoy proclaiming our truth!

Living in large, amiable pods, dolphins communicate with whistles, clicks, and body movements. Each pod has its dialect, and each dolphin its individual tone. Dolphin demonstrates the creative joy of communication, encouraging us to express our unique style as we turn dreams into reality.

In ancient times, Dolphin was a patron of sailors, a messenger from the water gods, a rescuer of shipwrecked souls. Dolphin holds knowledge of the deep sea, linking us to both planetary and inner oceans—and to expanded forms of awareness. Dolphin serves as a secret emissary from the stars, ambassador to other dimensions and worlds.

Dolphins also have a dark side. They can bully, harass, and kill. We often refuse to see this because we don't care to see it in ourselves. This, too, is part of Dolphin's medicine—to hold up a mirror to humanity, reminding us what it means to be fully human.

Dolphin encourages us to feel deeply and breathe, to play, dream, and love with abandon. Dolphin smiles as we let loose our natural exuberance with expressions of joy.

DOLPHIN SAYS

*Our connection with humanity is deep and vast. We help you to laugh.
We travel the inter-dimensional highways of being, moving through
many oceans —of both world and self —to reveal the healing power of joy.*

*We help you to connect your physical body with your deeper wisdom. We offer a link to other
worlds and different states of awareness. We are bridgers, connectors, friendly guides to trans-
dimensional meetings and creative cooperation.*

*Most of humanity needs to nurture a deep love of self. We work with joy and freedom and the
ecstasy of being. One of our main messages is to love yourself —deeply, truly —as you might
love us, entranced by our engaging smile, our delight in being dolphins. We hold and reflect the
projection of what you most love about yourself. We teach humans to swim in joy.*

Goat

Independent, agile, and inquisitive, goats are sure-footed adventure-seekers who love to climb. Nimble yet sturdy, mountain goats trek along high, craggy ledges, leaping great distances across chasms. Goat helps us to move forward, especially when we feel trapped or confused. With steady focus, Goat teaches us to look around, contemplate, consider our options. Goat shows us there is joy both in climbing high and in returning home.

Goat helps us to create a firm foundation, reminding us that success requires a strong center and stable base. Offering balance and flexibility, Goat prods us to explore new vistas and possibilities, as well as the unmapped terrain within. Moving with confidence, Goat urges us to stop worrying, thrill to adventure, and feel the excitement of joy.

Eager and curious, goats love to investigate. With prehensile lips and sensitive tongues, they feel and taste the world around them, finding hidden treasure in cans and jars, weaknesses in fences, and other ways in and out of adventure. Savvy and intelligent, Goat encourages us to follow our natural curiosity and sample everything—how else can we truly know the world?

Since goats are generous and gregarious animals, they are also versatile and accommodating. As one of the oldest domesticated species, they serve humans as a source of milk, cheese, meat, wool, and leather. In ancient sacrifice, we used goats as "stand ins" to appease the gods for our misconduct or immorality. The original scapegoat was a goat laden with human sins, cast into the wilderness alone.

Good-natured Goat gently pushes us to release guilt and other constraining emotions. Goat's deeper teaching, however, prods us to look within and accept responsibility for our thoughts and behavior. For Goat, finding oneself is the path to joy.

GOAT SAYS

Look within—that's our teaching about joy. We like to consider everything. Life's clues are all around us. We simply need to see. For humans, we sense you need to see within. That is the first lesson of clarity. If you can see clearly inside yourself, then you can also see clearly outside yourself. It works both ways, but our advice to humans is first to close your eyes and see within.

Our joy is roaming the world, exploring, being open to what we find. We appreciate beauty. We are dazzled by wonder. We like to look and contemplate, to stare into things—because a whole world lies behind appearances. Maybe this is why we tell you to look within. If you can see inside yourself, you will discover the joy of being yourself. Then you can share it with others. We are goats, peaceful advocates of joy!

Goldfish

Long associated with good luck and happiness, goldfish entrance us with their bright, shimmering colors, fluid movements, and long, filmy tails. Hardy and graceful, friendly and beautiful, goldfish symbolize contentment, peace, good fortune, and prosperity. Goldfish is a lighthearted teacher of joy.

Goldfish were domesticated in China over 1,000 years ago. Members of the carp family, they were originally raised for water gardens and ornamental ponds, and are able to balance home energies and to provide good feng shui.

Natural adaptors, goldfish thrive in diverse environments and mutate easily, aligning with our desire for brighter colors, unusual shapes, fancier tails. Goldfish readily complies. Spotted, multicolored or uniformly yellow, white, brown, black, bright orange, or red, goldfish delight us with their variations —fleshy hoods, shoulder humps, protruding eyes, double tails. We celebrate their surprising beauty with the names we give them: Black Moor, Bubble Eye, Fantail, Lionhead, Comet, and Butterfly Tail.

Connecting with goldfish is easy. Their keen visual acuity and awareness enables them to distinguish between colors, shapes, and human individuals. They learn our habits, follow movements against aquarium glass, and take food from our fingertips. Goldfish nurtures trust in the joy of simple things.

Sociable and engaging, goldfish help us to relax and find composure. Gliding through their watery domain, mesmerizing us with shimmering delicacy, goldfish spark our imagination and enliven our day dreams, leading us to altered perceptions and other realms.

With Goldfish calming our emotions and soothing our soul, we can swim happily through our creative world and feel at home in the peaceful tranquility of our inner sanctuary. Enchanting, radiant, fluid, and graceful, Goldfish spreads joy.

GOLDFISH SAYS

We dance. We express joy because we are joy. We feel joyful in the essence of our being.

We are accommodating because we love to share happiness, to awaken it in others, and to shine it wherever we go. We think of ourselves as little pieces of joy—colorful charms, stylish decorations, good friends, homey spirits. We can accommodate you—whatever you need, look to a goldfish.

We love to play with children, or the child inside of you. We can be elegant and radiant, quite sophisticated; or we can be plain old goldfish, teaching you to care for us—and so care for yourself, too.

We delight, we inspire, we swim within your heart. We will help you to smile, and that's one way to feel joy within. We dance. We share our wealth of joy with you.

Hummingbird

The smallest birds in the world, hummingbirds beat their wings faster than any other, and are also the only birds that can fly backward, as well as hovering and flying forward, sideways, and upside down. Each one visits over 1,000 flowers a day yet has no sense of smell. Surprising, magical, jewel-like expression of joy, tiny Hummingbird possesses a big spirit and potent medicine.

Ruby-throated, Violet-crowned, White-eared, Gilded, Green-bellied, Sparkling-tailed—the vibrant coloring of hummingbirds is reflected in the names of over 300 species, and their elaborate plumage includes crests, beards, streamer tails, and ruffs. Hummingbird feathers shimmer with iridescence, reminding us of life's brilliance.

Despite their delicate appearance, hummingbirds fight boldly, attacking intruders with their long, pointed beaks and beating wings. Their fearless, protective stance drives away much larger birds—a reason why they were once honored as courageous and lively warriors. Some hummingbirds fly hundreds of miles across water without eating—a feat once believed to be impossible. Hummingbird reminds us to be persistent and find joy through accomplishing our heart's desire, no matter the odds.

Hummingbirds spend most of their day flying from flower to flower in search of high-energy nectar. When cold or sleeping, they become dormant, almost lifeless. A symbol of resurrection and renewal of life, Hummingbird activates the warm glow of our inner sun, teaching us to open our hearts.

Inquisitive and opportunistic, hummingbirds cross-pollinate plants by sinking their long beaks into bright blooms, lapping nectar with their tongues. Intelligent and calculating, hummingbirds know which flowers they have visited and how long the flowers will take to refill with nectar.

Hummingbird teaches us to explore, adapt, savor the present moment, and appreciate the wonder and sweetness of life. With Hummingbird, we acknowledge the good in people. By sharing our feelings, we awaken their inner beauty and so spread the wealth of joy.

HUMMINGBIRD SAYS

We are small but spirited. We dart and move quickly, but we see clearly. Our medicine is fast and agile—a dash of beauty, a speck of joy, a flash of wonder. We move in and out of time, in-between the folds of your heart. We are a colorful blaze of magic.

We "hum" or buzz with energy that is too fine for you to see. Sometimes you can hear our healing, but other times you don't see or recognize us near. We often work invisibly, in the veils of spirit.

We can buzz inside your heart, quickening you to perceive the joy in life. This is what we do. We enliven, we inspire, we help you enjoy.

When we work with you, we move into you. In the same way that we enter the center of a flower, we come into your heart. And there we hum with joy.

Otter

Enthusiastic, energetic, and inquisitive, otters love to play, and in their eagerness to explore, they go wherever their curiosity leads them. Ever on the move, otters find ways to have fun in almost everything they do. Otter activates our sense of wonder, prodding us to awaken our inner child, and to play and swim joyfully through life.

Otters live in rivers, lakes, streams, and seas in many different parts of the world. Their long, sleek bodies, high energy, and strong, webbed feet mean they are well suited to aquatic environs. Lithe and limber, agile and acrobatic, otters chase, slide, dive, curl, swim, splash, and turn somersaults in the water. Naturally friendly, they enjoy company. Otter encourages us to welcome visitors, share our home, and celebrate with merriment.

Otters chuckle, purr, coo, twitter, squeal, and growl, communicating in a creative, free-spirited way. Otter guides us to loosen up, accept what comes, and express our feelings.

Whether diving, gliding, or floating on their backs, otters immerse themselves in the receptive, healing energies of water. Otter urges us to jettison fear and jealousy, to moderate our feelings with acceptance and love. Through their lively, amusing antics, otters go with the flow. Otter teaches us how to ride emotional ups and downs with supple grace.

Otter inspires curiosity, reminding us that life is immensely fascinating when approached with an open heart and mind. Otter is also a good problem-solver, helping us to detach from frustration as we arouse our natural sense of intrigue to investigate and find enlightening solutions.

With Otter as a guide, we renew our spirit and allow ourselves to be surprised. Otter reminds us to appreciate life, play, explore, and feed ourselves—often—with fun.

OTTER SAYS

We welcome life with an open heart. That is our teaching of joy. We don't care to fight or think of ways to change what is. When you accept your life, you can have fun and appreciate the present. Otter teaching is about attitude—how to embrace what is with a light heart and curious mind. We teach this to our pups from an early age. Explore! Discover! Look around! Isn't this fun?

We enjoy each other and our families, and everything around us—the plants and water and stones. We like to watch birds above and fish below. We love to glide through water—it is so welcoming, another aspect of joy!

Joy is something that is always present. This we know. It is up to you whether you choose to participate or not. Come join Otter for a little fun. We offer you a taste of joy.

Personal Power

GRASSHOPPER ~ HORSE ~ LION ~ PORCUPINE ~ SHARK

Real power flows freely, inspiring and invigorating without limit. When we are at peace with our authentic self, we feel good inside—safe, confident, and content. We recognize that the source of happiness comes not from "out there" but from within. Accepting responsibility for our thoughts and actions, we know we will find our way in the world, no matter the circumstance. Personal power comes from how well we know and love ourselves.

Centered in our power, we remain calm when others disagree with us. Gone is the need to coerce, compare, diminish, or judge. Freed from the desire to manipulate, we can assert ourselves without confrontation.

Healthy power is a balance—no need to bully; no need to fade away. Open to dialogue and differences, we find true wealth in relationships and experiences.

With power, we release control—and feel stronger. Authentic power brings resilience, courage, and integrity. By trusting and respecting ourselves, we feel secure. At ease with ourselves, ego ceases to rule. Status and possessions lose importance. We no longer need the outside world to validate or define us.

Expressing power, we feel our unique, brilliant, true flow. Whether conveyed through our passions, creations, thoughts, actions, or voice, personal power reminds us who we are—remarkable and magnificent. Finding our power can feel like coming home.

Experienced power often speaks softly. It teaches us about cooperation, and fine tunes our celebrations of love. Our heart opens, receptive and welcoming. We learn to ask questions that stimulate and strengthen the hidden power in others. Shining our power, we don't need to prove or convince. Rather, we encourage and motivate.

We can sometimes sense the depth of our power when we are still and observant. We feel ourselves pulse with the universe, our heartstrings thrumming in accord. Balanced power is achieved through unconditional love.

ANIMAL TEACHERS OF PERSONAL POWER

GRASSHOPPER ~ *Intuitive and mysterious, Grasshopper teaches that by trusting our perceptions and utilizing our inner power, we can leap forward impressive distances with ease.*

HORSE ~ *Running like the wind, full of adventurous spirit, Horse helps us to explore the wide range of our power through freedom, movement, and spiritual insight.*

LION ~ *Courageous and confident, Lion strengthens our spirit, helps us to express our authentic self, and reminds us to honor personal power both in ourselves and others.*

PORCUPINE ~ *Good-natured Porcupine encourages us to follow our path of power in peace, and allow others to travel theirs.*

SHARK ~ *Perceptive and innovative, intelligent survivor, guardian of hidden secrets, Shark guides us to deeper self-reliance, helping us to strengthen our power by gliding through our fears.*

Grasshopper

Ancient symbol of longevity, happiness, good luck, health, and abundance, Grasshopper helps us to leap forward in life by trusting our instincts and abilities. Some cultures viewed grasshoppers as noble signs of immortality or messengers of good news, while others sensed the personalities of deceased family members living within grasshoppers. When Grasshopper shows up, inspiration, change, and success are not far behind.

The several thousand species of grasshopper show unique variations—spotted, striped, clear winged, no winged, big headed, rainbow colored. All use their long, sensitive antennae to smell and feel the world. Grasshopper helps us to detect subtle energy and sharpen our intuition. With Grasshopper, we attune our perceptions, becoming more aware of our surroundings.

Pushing off with strong back legs, grasshoppers leap impressive distances—up to twenty times their length. Grasshopper nurtures forward thinking and speeds progress by reminding us to aim high. Grasshopper encourages us to trust our hunches and jump at chances that feel good.

Living in forests, grasslands, deserts, and mountains, grasshoppers commune with the earth and thus help us to ground and stabilize ourselves. By doing so, we can move forward fearlessly, vaulting across obstacles, into new places, situations, and dimensions. A master astral traveler, Grasshopper teaches that it's possible to jump across space and time—exploration via creative leaps and bounds.

Naturally clairvoyant, grasshoppers survey the big picture through their many-faceted compound eyes. Grasshopper expands awareness, helping us to integrate disconnected parts, to sense unity and the larger whole.

Grasshoppers communicate by rubbing their wings or legs together. By imitating their humming, buzzing sounds, ancient cultures altered consciousness—a powerful part of Grasshopper's medicine. With Grasshopper, we can access personal power by knowing when to sing, when to listen, and when to leap.

GRASSHOPPER SAYS

The power is in the push. You can't move forward unless you first feel it in yourself. This is our teaching about personal power.

We sense not only with our feelers, but also with our "gut"—a human analogy. For us, it is an empty, circular sensing space near our legs. We sense both within ourselves and, simultaneously, all around us. Imagine an invisible globe that expands to encompass everything in our environs.

Our sensing is quick and exact. When we feel the correct alignment between ourself and our position in space, we leap. We push and so express our power.

Our message is to feel deep inside yourself and also sense your placement within the world. Feel for proper alignment—the moment when you know the two to be the same. When you feel it, you will know. Then you can leap forward with the fullness of your power.

Horse

With beauty and grace, speed and stamina, Horse awakens the wild spirit within. Companion to the gods, symbol of freedom and power, horses often possess mystical qualities in myth and legend, appearing with extra legs, powerful wings, or a magic horn.

Associated with the wind and inner journeys, Horse accelerates intuitive understanding and deepens our spiritual path by leading us to graze on ancestral wisdom. Swift and determined, Horse hastens our journey through astral realms and helps us to maintain focus and stability in unfamiliar terrain. Horse brings latent abilities to light, encouraging us to discover the full depth and range of our power through the spirit of adventure.

Herd animals as well as strong-willed individuals, horses reveal how to relate lovingly to others yet maintain independence. Intuitive and compassionate, Horse excels in partnership. Teamed with Horse, we learn to develop balance, endurance, and skill, and to overcome obstacles. When horse and rider connect as one, we open to a larger adventure. Horse expands awareness of love, honor, loyalty, and friendship. With Horse, we gallop to spiritual awakening.

Horse activates wild, raw power, which can be difficult to control. When we abuse power or use it for personal gain and disregard others, the cost is high—for others and ourselves. By avoiding power, we don't move forward. Horse teaches us to use power constructively—to cultivate it in a positive way that empowers both others and ourselves.

Friendly and venturesome, Horse encourages us to follow our passion, find ourselves, and express the fullness of who we are. Horse reflects our yearning for the far reaches of adventure and the joy of freedom. With Horse, we learn to temper the immensity of our power with love.

HORSE SAYS

We are both strong and sensitive. This is our expression of personal power, although we feel "personal" power is inseparable from the power of all.

We feel deeply and know our place within the world—with our herd, in tandem with a mate, as mother to our young, or in relation to humans.

In our long history of association with humans, you have come to know our independent spirit as well as the way we acquiesce as work animals, or meet you as partners and friends.

We strive to lead with an open heart, to join with humans to share some of our wisdom, strength, and love. When we are running, we experience the thrill of freedom and joy. Humans experience this, too.

Our teaching to humanity is to open your heart and learn to live in balance with all life. To us, this is the highest teaching of personal power.

Lion

King of the jungle, lord of the beasts, symbol of the rising and setting sun, Lion has long been admired for physical prowess and spiritual wisdom. Associated with nobility, truth, and leadership, Lion signifies open-heartedness and courage. Lion's powerful presence reminds us to shine the radiance of our authentic self on the world.

Lions don't really live in jungles, but in African grasslands and savannas. Unlike many cats, they live in prides—an apt term to describe the way lions support each other and work together as loving, family teams. Male lions defend the pride's territory, while females hunt prey and rear the young. Lions are independent animals, and have strong personalities, but they ensure success by cooperating. Lion respects both male and female energies, and encourages us to honor both of these within ourselves.

Strong yet nurturing, playful yet fierce, lions expertly balance stillness and action, relaxation and work. Lion strengthens our spirit, showing us how to act with dignity in any situation. By displaying confidence and self-assurance, Lion teaches us to revere virtuous authority in ourselves and others, and to use power judiciously. With Lion, we reconnect with our wisdom and nobility.

Proud and watchful, lions take nothing for granted. They remain calm, fighting only when necessary, springing into action only when the time is right. Lion teaches us to avoid wasting energy on small things by observing carefully and wisely.

With its bold, fearless roar, Lion loudly proclaims the majesty of honor, dignity, pride, and self-respect. Lion reminds us to take heart, be courageous, and live our soul's purpose. This is how we become a sovereign being. In connecting with the depths of our power and revealing our true self, we rule our life with wisdom and balance.

LION SAYS

You call us king because you perceive within us a nobility of spirit, which you are often afraid to see within yourself.

Outwardly, we live as lions—eating, sleeping, hunting, loving, lounging in the sun. Yet we have an inner life as well. We are self-possessed, comfortable with our power, and embody this in both our inner and outer worlds.

Personal power is not for the faint of heart. Rather, it is about enlivening your heart, bringing life and inspiration into that most powerful of pumps within your body.

To be lionhearted means to be brave and daring, to have the courage to see yourself for who you are. We encourage you to explore your inner world with depth and acuity. We will walk with you, embolden you, help you to discover more about yourself.

Do you have the courage to approach us? We are Lion and we open our heart to you.

Porcupine

More than 30,000 quills cover a porcupine's body, but despite this bristly appearance, porcupines are good-natured and agreeable, defending only when frightened or threatened. Porcupine teaches us about protection and the proper use of personal power.

Porcupines live a simple, solitary life, exploring and foraging at night, making their way in the world. Porcupine advocates following a peaceful path, and allowing others to do the same.

Short-legged and slightly chunky, porcupines move at their own pace. They love to climb high and nestle in trees. Young porcupines often balance on their hind legs, rocking to and fro. Porcupine encourages us to find our natural rhythm. Secure in ourselves, we can relax and enjoy life, follow our passions and express our talents in unique, creative ways. Often curious and easily amused, Porcupine opens our heart to wonder and childlike innocence, reminding us to trust and have faith.

With excellent senses of hearing and smell, porcupines are keenly aware of others. They have few natural enemies, and so are generally confident and unafraid. It helps that their defense strategy surrounds them in the form of sharp, barbed quills. They flail and slap their tails at predators and overly curious animals who come too close. The quills detach easily but penetrate deeply and expand in the skin of the unlucky assailants, making the painful stingers difficult to remove. Porcupine teaches us how to shield ourselves from attack. Sensing this, traditional peoples often used quills as amulets or talismans to provide protection and repel negative energies.

Porcupine holds a calm, centered sense of personal power, reminding us to live and let live, but also encourages us to make our points stick, if need be. Porcupine medicine is quiet yet powerful.

PORCUPINE SAYS

We take it easy and enjoy our lives. We love our pups and teach them to take time to be aware of everything around us.

Our teaching about personal power is to be safe and secure inside yourself. We do not threaten or boast. When attacked, however, we will slap. It is our main defense and we are not afraid to use it. Our quills remind others to let us be.

Trust the peaceful path inside yourself. If others corner you, make your point known. But sometimes you just need to look prickly. Beneath our show, we are peaceful and nonaggressive. Does that surprise you?

We focus on ourselves—food, warmth, our babies, the natural progression of our life. Some would call this boring, but for us the world is full of wonder and delight. We are happy in ourselves. We are Porcupine.

Shark

Master of survival, Shark has dominated the oceans for hundreds of millions of years. Four hundred plus species of shark roam the seas. Many variations and specialties have evolved, and they thrive even in icy waters and at great depths. Curious, intelligent, innovative, and intuitive, Shark knows how to adapt, and has survived for eons by hunting and scavenging, clearing debris and caring for the ocean. Shark is an authority on living one's personal power.

Sharks have no swim bladder, and so must continually swim or risk sinking to the bottom of the sea. Thus they are ever alert and observant, and with keen, primal instincts, they skillfully seize their prey. Shark urges us to glide silently towards our goals, attentive to opportunity.

Shark—aloof, self-possessed, and in control—embodies mystery. We sometimes project derogatory meanings onto the word "shark," although it can also denote a talented and discerning expert. Sharply tuned senses enable sharks to detect energy grids and electric vibrations, and to smell distant prey. Shark guards ancient knowledge and secrets, prodding us to hone our instincts, so that we may realize how powerful we are.

Sharks are naturally calculating and highly perceptive, and they can discern situations quickly and clearly. Shark guides us deftly through our emotional waters, conflicts, and inner turmoils, without overwhelming us. With Shark, we gain composure and emotional wisdom.

The thought of sharks often ignites our fears, filling us with trepidation. These are the ultimate predators—their gaping mouths filled with all those sharp, pointed teeth. But sharks rarely attack humans, and many species of shark are docile. Shark encourages us to face our fears in order to identify what holds us back—usually ideas and beliefs rather than reality. Shark helps us to release irrational fears. With Shark, we mature in self-reliance and learn to express our inner power calmly and completely.

SHARK SAYS

We know who we are and what we want. For us, this is the essence of personal power.

When we work with humans, we eliminate the superfluous. We find humans mentally chatty and emotionally undefined. We teach streamlined wisdom. With us, you learn to think smoothly, feel clearly, and move cleanly through life.

We love the water, our home. We clean up after humans. We sense that you are often wasteful, irresponsible, and muddied in your approach to life, especially as you try to rationalize your debts to the earth.

We hold much wisdom but you continue to see us as frightful beasts. Until you can move past that, you have no business working with us. Our teaching is for those who desire to come clean, to sense beneath the human appearance of things. We help you to know yourself and what you want. We bring you back to personal power—a very good place to start.

Transformation

ALLIGATOR ~ BAT ~ BEETLE ~ BUTTERFLY ~ SNAKE

Birth and death, creation and destruction, beginnings and endings—transformation means a shift in form, character, nature, or status. One thing becomes another. To transform is to change.

Transformation bridges before and after, old and new. It can be an outer, physical change or a shift in how we perceive the world or experience ourselves. By transforming, we say goodbye to one way of life as we claim a fresh look or body, a different state of being or point of view.

Transformation can be as quick as lightning, surprising us, amazing us, changing everything in the blink of an eye. At other times, transformation is so slow and gradual we don't notice it occurring. It sneaks up on us as the years pass by.

Transformation can be secretive and magical. Think of a caterpillar forming a chrysalis. On the surface, everything is still and quiet, but inside all is aflutter. Then one day, a butterfly emerges. Transformation contains mystery as well as power.

In a still spot in the center of transformation, we are betwixt and between—not what we were, but not yet what we will become. In that space we touch the infinite expansiveness of creative potential.

Some transformation feels difficult, and can be scary. We may not want to change or we may fear the process, clinging to the familiar. All that we know seems to slide away, leaving us with—what? But transformation can be joyous, too—a birth, a sudden inspiration, enlightenment, a new way to see the world. Transformation can encourage and inspire, enliven our hearts, uplift our souls.

With transformative processes at work, old paradigms no longer satisfy us as our perspective broadens and our consciousness expands. The outer world remains the same, but our perception alters so dramatically that it is as if we see another world, which, of course, we do.

Transformation writ large is evolution—a parade of changing species, the ever-shifting form of our planetary face, leaps of consciousness, awakenings, and sudden understanding. In transformation, endless possibilities abound.

ANIMAL TEACHERS OF TRANSFORMATION

ALLIGATOR ~ *Guardian of ancient wisdom, protector of primal energies, Alligator initiates those who are ready to access hidden knowledge of self and soul.*

BAT ~ *Shy, winged creature of the night, Bat teaches us to see in the dark and release our fear of change. Bat pollinates new ideas and awakens new ways of being.*

BEETLE ~ *For variety and sheer abundance, Beetle amazes us. Linked to immortality and the center of the universe, Beetle opens our mind to larger perspectives and the renewal of life.*

BUTTERFLY ~ *Butterfly reminds us to trust the rhythms of nature and welcome the creative process of change. With Butterfly, we learn to spread our wings and fly when the time is right.*

SNAKE ~ *Awakening dormant energies and unlocking hidden knowledge, Snake brings spiritual transformation, and heals through change.*

Alligator

Intelligent, astute, self-possessed, prehistoric predators, alligators are the largest reptiles on earth, our last living link to the age of dinosaurs. They are also strong and powerful. Alligator employs keen skills and instincts to guard primal energies and ancient wisdom. Alligator medicine is fierce and deeply transformative. Attentive to birth and death, creation and destruction, Alligator leads us deep within ourselves to face our fears, but initiates only those who are ready to retrieve hidden knowledge and sacred secrets of the self.

Alligators' eyes and nostrils are positioned high on the head, so they can watch what happens above the water while hiding beneath the surface. Acutely sensitive, alligators see well both underwater and at night. Alligator helps us to perceive clearly without being seen.

Concealed, motionless, in mud or water, alligators wait patiently for the right moment — to snap! They may swallow prey whole or stash it beneath submerged branches to eat later. Alligator reminds us to waste nothing and assess the best way to absorb and digest our experiences fully before moving on.

Tough, scaly skin helps with camouflage and armoring, but an alligator's belly is soft and vulnerable. Alligator protects and defends, yet is open to life's emotional undercurrents. Fearless, forthright, and exacting, Alligator demands full attention and focus, prompting us to see things as they are, not as we want them to be.

Alligators are comfortable both on land and in water. In either environment, they move efficiently, wasting no effort. Alligator helps us to remain grounded while navigating cleanly through emotional waters, showing us precisely how to hold our own and detect deceit, especially when subject to the ruses of drama and manipulation.

Alligator opens us to rebirth and offers strength to create new opportunities. By connecting us with our own deep knowledge, Alligator guides us to the source of originality, wisdom, and life.

ALLIGATOR SAYS

Our advice to humans? Stop making us into belts and boots. What do you think you are doing wearing alligator? You admire our power but have no real connection, using us in such superficial ways. This is a game you play with yourselves.

Those who really want to work with Alligator will intensify their understanding. Our power is nestled inside your sacral center, the seat of survival and primordial knowledge.

In former times, we worked with humans through grand initiations, taking you deep into your power, awakening ancestral memories, serving as guardian and teacher, advisor and guide. To wear alligator in those days meant something. We were connected, joined in common focus of planetary awakening.

We do not care to wrestle with humans or be worn as adornments. If you are serious about our wisdom, we are here. You need only sink down into yourself and see. We are Alligator, watching you from within.

Bat

Emerging at twilight from dark caves or shadowy roosts, stretching their wings to the night sky, bats are the only mammals that can fly. Associated with darkness, the underworld, and death as well as good luck, blessings, and the immortal soul, bats bewilder us with their unusual traits. Powerful initiators and symbols of rebirth, Bat signals the flight of one life and the transition to another.

Some bats are shy and secretive, living alone, while others congregate in huge underground colonies, with special nurseries for mothers and pups. These sociable bats have strong family ties, nurturing by touch and gentle interaction.

Bats are generally underappreciated, despite being highly beneficial to humans and the natural world. Most bats eat insects—an average colony can devour several tons each night. Some eat nectar and fruit, pollinating plants as they move from flower to flower. Others catch fish and frogs, and still others feed on animal blood. There are more than 1,000 species of bats—diverse, unique, and intelligent.

Bats have small eyes and nocturnal habits, but they are not blind. Some bats rely on their eyesight, although most emit high-frequency sounds and use echolocation to hunt and navigate accurately through the dark. Bat helps us to hone our perceptions, sense our surroundings, and discern hidden messages. Bat greatly enhances night vision and dreaming.

As a creature of the night, Bat guides us through our darkest fears. Bat advises us to let go of the superfluous, which, at times, may feel like death. Prompting us to look past illusion, however, Bat transforms fear into power, initiating new ideas and visions—different ways of being. When we confront our inner demons and release deep-seated fear patterns, we are reborn.

Bat medicine is potent and long-lasting. It takes us to extremes, encouraging us to fulfill our higher potential. Bat demands commitment and likewise commits to those willing to risk the journey.

BAT SAYS

We are at home in the dark. Thus we can teach you much about seeing and moving when light is in short supply. For us, the dark is not a place of fear but a source of power. The dark can nurture and lead you deeper within.

We often guide humans to inner caverns where you can contemplate in stillness. We teach different ways to transmute and transform. We are highly creative, innovative, and resourceful. We know how to adapt and are good at figuring out solutions.

We mostly work with humans who are ready to make dramatic changes. Ours is an intense study. It requires some focus—and desire—to peer deeply into the darkness within.

Our teaching about transformation is: Shifts happen. It is up to you whether to take advantage of the natural openings and opportunities to change. Some are easy and gentle. Others take you way down. We help with deep transformation. We are Bat.

Beetle

The most varied and numerous of all insects, beetles have lived on earth for 300 million years. With over 350,000 different forms, beetles are hugely successful, comprising one quarter of our planet's life forms. Beetles live almost everywhere, in diverse habitats, but most abundantly in tropical rainforests. Some beetles shine like brilliant jewels, while others are masters of camouflage. Beetle teaches change, adaptation, perseverance, and the marvels of multiplicity.

Coleoptera—the scientific name for beetles—means "sheathed wing" and describes the lightweight, hardened pair of fore wings that shield flight wings. Beetles amaze and mystify. Fireflies glow at night; water beetles submerge inside air bubbles; and ladybugs, symbols of good fortune and happiness, enchant children, and help gardeners by eating aphids. Beetles can devastate forests and fields of cotton and potatoes. They also pollinate flowers, improve soil conditions, and keep insect populations in balance. Beetle reminds us that "good" or "bad" depends on our perspective. Beetle celebrates distinctions and embraces abundant variations.

Like many insects, beetles completely transform their body structure through metamorphosis—transitioning from egg to crawling grub to winged adult. Beetle helps us to pace ourselves through dramatic change, and shows the necessity of releasing the old in order to give birth to the new. Beetle is an expert at transformation and renewal.

The scarab beetle, held sacred by the ancient Egyptians, symbolizes resurrection. Scarabs were used as protective amulets and placed with the mummified dead as a sign of continued life in the next world. Alchemists regarded scarabs as guides to the center of the universe.

As a guardian of the path to immortality, Beetle holds knowledge of past and future lives. By enticing us to see wider perspectives, Beetle helps us to trust the process of change and relax into transitions from life to death and beyond. Beetle harmonizes changes and helps us to transform consciously.

BEETLE SAYS

We delight in our many forms. We are ancient and yet continually renewing ourselves — evolving and adapting and changing. Many more species of us exist than humans know. That, too, is part of our mystery.

We teach patterns of change. We can help you learn to transition, especially in dramatic ways, but also share our knowledge of evolving new and different forms.

Our nature is innovative, inquisitive, and aesthetic. We are speaking broadly here, as Spirit of Beetle. Some of our species are very focused and do not change much. But as a whole, we continually reshape ourselves and embrace new adaptations.

We enjoy working with humans who are both scientific and creative. Not many humans consider us, but those who do know we have much to teach. We celebrate the joy of diversity and the creative nature of transformation. We are Beetle!

Butterfly

BEAUTY ~ JOY ~ PATIENCE ~ TRUST ~ TRANSFORMATION WITHOUT TRAUMA

Colorful symbol of joy and transformation, Butterfly reminds us to trust the process of change. Often associated with awakening and rebirth, Butterfly begins life as a crawling caterpillar, hides within a mysterious, closed chrysalis, then unfurls, wide winged and glorious. Butterfly encourages us to have faith. By witnessing the magic of change, we perceive the inspiring, creative possibilities of who we may become.

Butterflies enliven the world with delicate beauty and wonder. Smelling with their antennae, tasting with their feet, drinking nectar with their long proboscis, butterflies feel vibrations and see ultra-violet light shimmering on flowers. Weighing no more than a few flower petals, butterflies can fly thousands of miles in migration. Butterfly awakens us to magic, helps us to sense the overall picture—often in unexpected ways—and to remain consciously attuned to our surroundings.

Patient, sensitive to timing and environmental harmony, butterflies dance with the flow of life. Laying their eggs on plants that will provide food for newly hatched caterpillars, butterflies teach us to nurture our ideas. Caterpillars molt several times—a reminder that new growth may require repeatedly shedding the old and outgrown. A caterpillar's final molt into a chrysalis creates a safe space for rapid change. But signs of deep change may not be immediately apparent. Butterfly encourages patience, suggesting the wisdom of waiting.

Butterfly fosters sensitivity, helping us to identify our transitional stage and adjust to the next accordingly. Butterfly neither hurries nor holds on, but rather, inspires us to trust our instincts, rest when necessary, and break loose when it is time to fly.

Butterfly reminds us that transformation is a natural process and need not be frightening or traumatic. Change can occur gently, with grace and joy. Butterfly boosts self-esteem and confidence, cheering us on to love our life and trust the rhythm of change.

BUTTERFLY SAYS

We are creatures of light and warmth. We enjoy the fullness of our being.

Our teaching about transformation is to relax. That's right—take time to breathe deeply and allow the change that is upon you.

Part of the reason we seem so happy-go-lightly is that we have gone through much of our transformation before we awaken as butterflies. Our butterfly appearance is the aftermath of our deepest change, and so we are light and beautiful.

Our gift to the world is to inspire and uplift, to remind you that much beauty comes with change. Consider the cramped darkness of our internal change—we enclose ourselves and die in one form. But we trust completely, and are born again.

You did not know Butterfly teaching was so deep? We dance around you, flutter through your heart. If in fear, imagine a butterfly. We will be near. We grace the world with love.

Snake

Linked to creation, wisdom, rebirth, and transformation, Snake is a symbol of wholeness and immortality. Both feared and worshipped, snakes often mystify humans. Is a snake the bearer of temptation, malevolence, and death, or an energetic initiator, healer, and muse? Where sexuality is celebrated, Snake is honored, but where sexuality is feared, Snake is disparaged or demonized. Snake coils and wraps, slithers and slides. Snake represents the sensual flow of energy that keeps us alive.

The nearly 3,000 species of snake may differ in shape, color, and size, but all are flexible, moving with agility and grace. Smelling with a flickering tongue, seeing with eyes that are always open, hearing low-frequency sounds without external ears, snakes perceive secret underworld mysteries. Versatile and highly attuned to vibrations, Snake connects us with deep, untapped power and helps us to heal on the cellular level.

Just as snakes periodically shed their skin, Snake urges us through transformation, prompting us to shed the old and embrace the new. Snake brings dramatic change by expediting the release of outgrown beliefs, illusions, and limitations.

Before molting, snakes stop eating and hide. As its outer skin dulls and separates from the new skin underneath, the snake's transparent eye scales turn opaque, suggesting trance or astral travel. Wriggling from its skin, journeying out of its body, the snake emerges as a new being. Encompassing birth and death, Snake transforms through the wisdom of experience.

Generally calm and peaceful, snakes are slow to anger, but within their coils lies immense power. When provoked, snakes strike with precision and control. Sharpening our intuition, accelerating spiritual understanding, Snake requires both respect and attention.

Snake opens us to new growth by connecting us with primordial life energies and awakening deep creative forces. As guardian to the sacred spaces within our soul, Snake unlocks hidden knowledge and initiates spiritual transformation. Snake encircles the fullness of life.

SNAKE SAYS

We hold mystery and this is one of the reasons why many humans fear us. We don't take it personally. We are Snake—wide ranging, diverse, knowledgeable, and wise.

We are deep initiators and tend to work with humans individually. We are deepeners. We often lead you into change bit by bit, nudging you slowly to become comfortable with it. Our deepest work, however, is quick and sudden—and irreversible.

At a certain point you meet Snake as Guardian—the one who both nurtures and protects your deepest secrets. Our wisdom lies in waiting for the right moment of awareness. We sense openings in humans and then we act. We can lead you within to find your treasure—or, in fear, you can run away.

When you are open, you see us for who we are. When you can stand your ground and look us in the eye, you are ready for our teaching.

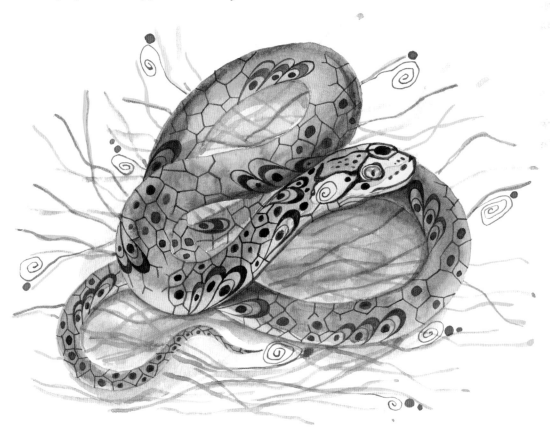

GROUP 12

Wisdom

MOOSE ~ OWL ~ SPIDER ~ TURTLE ~ WHALE

Wisdom is gentle and kind. It speaks softly and bides its time. Hard to measure, teach, capture, or confine, wisdom flows and permeates. It doesn't always make sense, but we recognize it when we feel it. It resonates within. When we are infused with its presence, we know the essential truth of life.

We cannot buy wisdom, but sometimes it is offered freely. Wisdom is born of good sense and accumulated knowledge and experience. It is much more than mere information or familiarity with current events. Still, any detail of life with a gleam of significance, a sparkle of meaning, can lead us deeper and on to the extraordinary. Wisdom beckons and twinkles in the everyday.

Engaged in the pursuit of wisdom, we may access ancient knowledge, sacred teachings, expansive and eternal views. Open to our instincts, trusting our feelings, we perceive interconnection, the magical composition of life. Connecting the dots in the starlit sky, we sense vastness within ourselves. Content and spiritually connected, we know there is endless space and opportunity for wisdom to grow.

Opening our minds, we embrace contradiction, paradox, mystery. We need no intermediaries to dictate truth, no prescribed rules, tenets, methods, or plans. Rather, we learn through experience, the master teacher. Wisdom often comes from failure. Being wise, we do not despair. We understand this well-worn route to wisdom.

We may glean wisdom by observation or reflection. Alert to feelings, welcoming insights, following the wise paths left by others, we quicken inner awakening. Some wisdom comes with tears of difficulty, sadness, grief—the hard-edged teaching of experience may change our life. With maturity comes balance, perspective, and tranquility.

Wisdom rarely offers explanations, allowing us to see or hear, or not. With wisdom, we discern, intuit, and act appropriately. In the heat of emotion, we remember to breathe. With wisdom, we feel whole. We know our home in the delicate, dew-draped web of life. Bestowing a calming presence and depth of knowing, wisdom curls in the center of our heart with love.

ANIMAL TEACHERS OF WISDOM

MOOSE ~ *A no-nonsense teacher with strong ties to ancient knowledge, Moose champions confidence and common sense. Moose reminds us to stay true to ourselves and value our inherent wisdom.*

OWL ~ *Perceptive shadow guide and talented nocturnal hunter, Owl teaches us to sense clearly so we may act with swiftness and precision. Guiding us through the dark, Owl shows us the path to inner wisdom.*

SPIDER – *Spider reminds us that we are responsible for weaving our reality with fate. Nurturing communication, connection, and artistic design, Spider illuminates the ancient wisdom of creation.*

TURTLE ~ *Tranquil and patient, Turtle helps us to move steadily through life's up and downs. Turtle advocates persistence, peaceful protection, and introspective wisdom.*

WHALE ~ *Guiding us to deep, vast wisdom within, Whale awakens and empowers us, attuning us to love. Whale sounds the heartbeat of universal connection.*

Moose

Humped shoulders, a burly torso, lanky legs, big ears, flapping dewlap, and a bulging nose give moose an appearance that is both imposing and ungainly. Generally slow and unhurried, moose can move with surprising speed and agility, and they are able to call on reserves of strength and stamina when traversing deep snow, water, and rugged terrain. Symbol of endurance, practical wisdom, and steadfast determination, Moose balances power with sensibility, reminding us that not all is as it seems.

The largest member of the deer family, moose spend their days foraging alone or with their calves. Wandering through northern forests and tundra, grazing on grasses, shrubs, and trees, moose find food, even in harsh winters. Male moose grow enormous antlers each year. Attuned to ancient wisdom and experience, Moose awakens psychic abilities and grants access to hidden knowledge.

Acute senses of smell and hearing enable moose to be well aware of others. Stomping, snorting, or calling loudly, moose know when to make their presence known—and also when to move unseen. Insightful and alert, Moose watches before acting, prompting us to do the same.

Moose are fond of aquatic plants, and often stand knee-deep in lakes and ponds, submerging their large heads to munch. Associated with receptive, feminine energies, Moose nudges us to dip below the surface and discover hidden nourishment within.

Undaunted and resolute, moose jump fences and cross highways to forge ahead. Moose encourages us to stay true to ourselves and attain our goals by staying focused and determined, transcending boundaries when needed. Moose's outlook is a wide-ranging balance of hardiness and sensitivity.

Moose urges us to value our strengths and achievements, reinforcing self-esteem and confidence, and inspiring celebration of accomplishment—not to show off, but to share joy and motivate others. Moose encourages us to trust, honor, accept, and love ourselves. This is Moose's wisdom.

MOOSE SAYS

For us, wisdom is a centered presence of safety, knowledge, wonder, and love. As we wander, we deepen our awareness by connecting with the land. Through wandering, our territory becomes well known—and loved. We never feel alone.

We work with other animals, sometimes humans, although not so much with thoughts. We teach through presence and feeling, through assuredness that comes from intense, loving association with the land.

We travel not only across the land, but also, with our mind and feelings, into the earth. It is an adventure of consciousness to sink into the land and converse with earth guardians. We anchor our wisdom in this way.

We can help you to find elder wisdom and read the records of earth changes. But mostly we help you to search within yourself and find your own connection. From there the journey is up to you.

Owl

Skilled night hunters, both respected and feared, owls are linked with the moon and spirit world, and are often regarded as omens, bringers of magic and prophecy. Owl guards the nocturnal mysteries that surround us, whether we choose to see them or not. Perched on Athena's shoulder, Owl lends night vision to the goddess of wisdom.

Owl is a messenger, a holder of secret knowledge, and welcomes its shadow self. Seeing through deception, Owl perceives what others miss. Owl leads us into the dark unknown, reminding us to open our eyes and attune our senses, teaching us to perceive inner wisdom and follow its guidance.

The hundred-plus species of owl vary in size and abilities, from the five-inch, cactus-dwelling Elf Owl to the Great Horned Owl, which has huge, furry talons, a five-foot wingspan, and the ability to fly faster than an eagle. Master predators, owls eat insects, fish, rodents, and small mammals, serving as ecological balancers. Owl clears away the overwhelming and out of control.

Extraordinary vision and keen hearing enable owls to notice subtleties in their surroundings, especially in the dark. On soft, thick wings they glide silently through the air and then suddenly swoop on prey. Owl teaches stealth, secrecy, and swift movement. Reliable truth-teller, Owl helps us to sense with clarity and precision.

Screeching, whistling, hooting and calling, owls are occasionally heard, though not often seen. Owl teaches the value of silent contemplation, balancing quiet composure with decisive action.

Listen! Watch! Be patient! Discern! Owl teaches us to find and follow our inner counsel. By piercing illusions, Owl extracts secrets, nudging us to see behind the scenes, under the surface, in the dark, in the depths of our being. Owl offers accurate vision and clear navigation through dreams, fears, and repressed emotions. Owl teaches us to pay attention to our perceptions—this is how we gain wisdom.

OWL SAYS

We are birds of wisdom. We know what we want and we take it when the time is right. We teach clarity of vision and precise action attuned to the harmony of life. Our wisdom focuses on vision and movement because we bring the two together.

We see through the folds of reality. By seeing beyond the surface, through the apparent and deeper into the alignment of all things, we appreciate the larger picture. We apprehend what is properly aligned and so we act. We know our place in the cycle of life. That, too, is part of our wisdom.

We are called Wise Owl because we carry an ancient wisdom. We reflect the truth of things.

We sometimes fly with humans in dreams and visions. We are very loving, which is not often recognized. We welcome you to see with Owl eyes. Then you will know. We are happy to share our gifts of wisdom.

Spider

Symbol of mystery and wisdom, protector of the primordial design of creation, Spider may be small but its medicine is powerful. In mythology, Spider appears as both creator and trickster—spinning worlds, weaving fates, snaring the unsuspecting and unmindful. Loyal keeper of earth wisdom, Spider reminds us that we weave reality by our thoughts and actions, and for this we are responsible.

Ancient peoples perceived meaning within the threaded lines, angles, and patterns of spiders' webs. This is how Spider inspired the alphabet. Guardian of ancient languages, symbols, and sacred messages, Spider fosters communication, translation, and interpretation. Spider awakens imagination and nurtures creativity, encouraging us to imbue expression with artistry and design.

Found in most parts of the world, spiders number more than 35,000 species, all of which amaze and mystify. Generally solitary, spiders have eight legs and some have eight eyes. All spiders are predators, although not all of them weave webs. Wolf spiders stalk their prey, trapdoor spiders wait in burrows, and tarantulas paralyze with venom. Web-weaving spiders create patterns that vary by species, forming funnels, tangles, sheets, domes, and orbs.

Alluring, magical, Spider's web displays integration, harmony, and sacred geometry. Delicate yet incredibly durable, spider silk is pound-for-pound five times stronger than steel. Spiders create webs by linking thread to silken thread, forming a frame that expands and connects. Sensitive to vibration, spiders detect movement anywhere on the web. Spider helps us to focus yet stay responsive to life as we spin our plans.

Intimately connected with earth teachings, Spider promotes balance and respect. Weaving together past and future, physical and spiritual, Spider spins a web of unity and uses the secrets of creation to remind us how strongly the web of life joins us all. By making responsible choices and owning our power, we find our center and feel our interconnection and wholeness—a gift born of Spider's wisdom.

SPIDER SAYS

We teach trust. We trust that each new day will come. For us, trust is a path to wisdom. Our teaching to humanity is about trusting yourself. You have a great deal of power to affect your world, your life, each new day. We spiders delight in boundless creation, ongoing design, and endless weaving of reality. We support continuing education! We urge you to take time to notice the details in your life. As our webs attest, the delicate and small is often incredibly strong.

For us, wisdom is found within. A power spot in our center, an inner space — you have it, too — connects us to infinity. This is where we spin our silk, a kind of umbilical cord that signifies our connection to creation. In ancient times, we inspired poets and painters, gave counsel to emperors and kings. No one suspects this of a little spider, but we do big things. Trust!

Turtle

Turtles have walked and swum on earth since before the age of dinosaurs. They live for up to 150 years, symbols of tranquility and persistence. Ancient peoples believed their longevity, survival skills, and placid existence were signs of wisdom. Turtle travels a patient, prudent, peaceful path, secure in its sense of self and in its centered knowledge.

In many mythologies, Turtle carries creation upon its back. Its shell equates to the vault of heaven, its body the earth, and its belly the underworld. Turtle shells often served as instruments of divination, revealing secret star maps and sacred writings to those who paid attention.

The 250 species of turtle vary in form and habitat. Sea turtles have light, streamlined shells, and long, webbed feet that they use as flippers to swim and glide. Land turtles, or tortoises, have heavier, protective shells, stumpy legs and nubby feet for walking, and sharp claws for digging. Freshwater turtles may live on land or water; many have webbed feet like sea turtles but hard shells like tortoises. Attuned both to land and water energies, Turtle safeguards earth wisdom and patrols the sea. Turtle helps us to stay grounded and paddle smoothly through emotional waters.

Most turtles are able to retract head, limbs, and tail and so hide inside their shell in times of danger. Turtle shields and protects non violently. There are times to stick out our neck and times to withdraw. Turtle encourages us to retreat when we feel threatened—thus we may contemplate our next move and find answers within. Turtle reveals the wisdom of introspection.

Traveling close to the earth, carrying its home wherever it goes, Turtle reminds us to honor our world and soak in its nurturing, healing love. Deepening our senses to nature's rhythm, appreciating our life, and taking time to enjoy our journey is how we follow the path of Turtle's wisdom.

TURTLE SAYS

We feel deep connection with Mother Earth. Our teaching is about finding harmony within yourself and with our world. By doing so, you make the planet a better place for others as well as for yourself. To us, this is both loving and wise.

Each turtle species has a separate teaching, offering wisdom from its own place. Some hold sacred space within the oceans—many turtles are stewards for planetary awakening and many anchor light stations within water. Other turtles hold wisdom on land or between land and water. Turtles get around!

What we suggest to humans is to find more depth. For us, wisdom is not accumulated knowledge, but feeling deep connection. Wisdom grows through experience.

We often draw upon "Old Turtle"—or "Ancestral Turtle"—to tap into wisdom. We sink down and listen; we open ourselves and remember. Wisdom speaks softly at times. Listen with your heart. That is our suggestion. We are Turtle. We abide in peace.

Whale

Whales inspire awe and wonder. Revered for their massive presence and elegant movement, ancient peoples thought them living islands, water gods, wise guardians of the oceanic realm.

Powerful swimmers with strong fins and sturdy tails, whales travel long distances. Humpbacks, bowheads, and blue whales, the largest animal known, are famous for singing, and move in small pods or alone, while sperm whales, belugas, and the magnificently tusked narwhal are smaller and more social. As sea mammals, all whales must surface to breathe. When diving, they link us to personal and planetary depths. Leaping skyward, they connect earth to heaven. Whale stimulates imagination and exploration, urging us to access creative power and magic within.

Intelligent, sensitive, and highly perceptive, Whale navigates emotional healing, bringing repressed feelings, fear, and trauma to the surface. Whale encourages us to move through emotional holds consciously and with love.

Whale songs offer sacred frequencies that expand awareness and allow travel to other worlds and dimensions. Sounding the call to cosmic consciousness, Whale awakens us, nudging us to feel the pulse, the heartbeat of the universe.

As record keepers, whales hold ancient memories, knowledge, and wisdom. Whale grounds and opens, accelerating psychic awareness, urging us to trust our feelings and know that we, too, are wise. Whale guides us to perceive wonder in the world. Family oriented and nurturing, whales form close, loving relationships. Whale promotes wellbeing, teaching us to remain aware and trust the unknown as we swim into the vastness of our being. Whale dreams large, attuning us to love, the deepest form of wisdom.

WHALE SAYS

We hold a depth of planetary healing and we resound the tone of love for all. What we most want to tell humans is to love yourselves. We find you have a hard time with this.

We whales know our magnificence and so see magnificence in you as well. We call to you to awaken to your vast power and dormant love.

If you swim with us or watch us, you will feel love. We invite you to relax into the depth of your being, to join us inside your being.

Our advice to you is simple—love. Let go of all that hardens your heart and weighs you down. We are buoyant and large because we hold an immensity of peace and contentment within.

Whale wisdom is no different from your own, for we are you. Feel the presence of whale inside yourself and you will know. We call to share love with you.

Index

Acknowledgments

Thanks to my husband Bob and daughter Alyeska for their love and understanding, especially while I worked on this book. Thanks to friend and writer Phil Kotofskie for helpful suggestions on improving the text. Thanks to Cindy Richards, Dawn Bates, Marion Paull, Sally Powell, Paul Tilby, Jerry Goldie, Ingrid Court-Jones, Michele Clarke, and all the good people at CICO Books. Thanks to artist Ola Liola for her remarkable illustrations that convey so much animal energy. And many thanks to all of the animals who participated in this book, lending their wisdom, humor, insights, guidance, and compassion. Together, we create a more wonderful world.